How not to be a diplomat

How not to be a diplomat

Adventures in the Indian Foreign Service Post-Independence

By P.L. Bhandari

How not to be a diplomat

P.L. Bandhari

Published by The Quince Tree Publishing Ltd

P.L. Bhandari has recreated events, locales and conversations from his memories of them. In order to maintain anonymity in some instances, individual names and places have been changed. He also may have changed some identifying characteristics and details such as physical properties, characteristics and places of residence.

Cover artwork by

Marta Munoz

www.martamunoz.co.uk

Cover design by

Andy Irvine Park

www.andypark.net

ISBN 978-0-9576979-0-4

10 9 8 7 6 5 4 3 2 1

the Quincetree

Company number: 05928801

info@thequincetree.co.uk

www.thequincetree.co.uk

About the author

P.L.Bhandari was born in Lahore in 1911, the eldest of four children. After leaving Government College in Lahore, where he trained as a journalist, he joined The Civil and Military Gazette, a local newspaper, where Rudyard Kipling penned many a tale. In the early 1940s he became a publicity officer in The War Services Exhibition, and in 1945, became Information Officer to Canada, a post designed to introduce India to the far corners of the Empire.

In 1947, when India became independent, he was asked to join the newly formed Indian Foreign Service, where he remained through postings in London, The Hague, Washington, and Djakarta. In 1956 he was to be posted to the newly independent Ghana, but at the last minute this was changed, and he was sent to head the council in Lahore, which subsequently closed down due to trouble between India and Pakistan.

He then went on a home posting to New Delhi, until, in 1960, he became India's Ambassador to Mexico. In 1964 he was sent as a High Commissioner to Nigeria, and ended his career as a diplomat after serving as High Commissioner to the Sudan.

After his retirement from the Foreign Service he lived in Calcutta, where he returned to his first love – writing. He wrote three books of short stories, which were published in India, he also wrote for many national newspapers and magazines. Some of his stories have been published by the B.B.C World Service and Readers Digest.

HOW NOT TO BE A DIPLOMAT

Introduction

Preface

How to be a diplomat   1

How not to be a diplomat   22

Embrace your gifts   32

Observe people   44

Celebrate your community   71

On the family   90

Epilogue

INTRODUCTION

I first met Rowena Sagrani (née Bhandari) through a mutual friend who suggested that we might be able to work together. Rowena had in her possession a pile of manuscripts written by her late father and she had been looking for someone to help her turn them into a publishable book. The material consisted of a large number of short stories and musings about his and other people's lives. Some of it had been previously published in one form or another, though for the most, the stories remained unedited and unpublished.

A number of things struck me about Bhandari's writings: the authenticity of his language; his suspension between the Western and Eastern values, and his own personal fallibility, all place him as a unique character in a period of enormous social change.

At a time when India was a new country and high on the international agenda, PL Bhandari and his playboy image works hard to debunk the stereotype of the aesthetic Indian. Possibly as a result of which, we get the feeling that he may have been demoted towards the end of his working life, although it may not actually have been himself that was to blame. Already the more professionalized diplomat was coming in and with it, the challenging eccentricities of a by-gone era, lost through our modern sobriety.

The material contained within has been very lightly edited – my main work has been to compile the stories. I have also added some footnotes, to aid the reader through some of the terminology used.

Natasha Muñoz

PREFACE

Jawaharlal Nehru was the hero of my generation, idolised like no other, not even Mahatma Gandhi. Each one of us would gladly have faced a firing squad at his command. We discussed him daily, with reverence yet with familiarity because, after all, were we not comrades-in-arms? Yet I was tongue-tied when I met him for the first time.

We were sitting around a small table in one of the salons of the Hotel Royal Monceau in Paris, where our delegation was staying. He had come to address the third session of the United Nations General Assembly, then being held at the Palais de Chaillot. India had newly become independent and this was his debut as Prime Minister before an international audience.

He looked around the table and said to no one in particular: "I envy you" and I remember asking him: "Why do you envy us, Sir?"

His eyes rested on me for a long moment, and then he replied: "Because you are Indians and India has been re-born. You are members of its Foreign Service and excitement awaits you in every nook and corner of the far-flung world in which you will serve. New horizons beckon: every day will be an adventure. You will have the honour and the responsibility of representing a new-old country and explaining its dreams and ambitions and removing at least some of the many misconceptions that exist about it. There will be obstacles and challenges to overcome – but what would life be without its challenges?" He paused, then said softly: "Ah, to be young again!"

It was exactly as he had predicted. In those days an Indian diplomat was pampered and privileged beyond his status. Mostly everyone looked up to him; many wanted to shelter him. Each day brought fresh problems, fresh experiences, but always there was the urge to get on with the job. Wordy battles were fought in chancelleries and conference halls, some important, others not so important, all demanding undivided attention. It was the headiest moment of our history.

Throughout this book, no attempt has been made to pronounce judgements on our foreign policy or to comment on its conduct. My endeavour has been solely to entertain – myself and (hopefully) the reader.

PL Bhandari

1

How to be a diplomat

"How does one become a diplomat?" I am often asked and, of course, there is no simple answer – it entirely depends on the age in which you live. Nowadays, the obvious way is to sit for the Foreign Service entrance examination, come out high up on the list, and then, for the rest of your life, imbibe and practice all the arts and wiles that have earned for diplomacy every epithet under the sun.

I will refer to an acquaintance I recently happened upon for a description of the diplomatic service in the old days – "In the old days" he says, "before you even had a service, there was no fuss about grades and exams. All you needed to get into the Diplomatic world was to be a youth of a good family with a private income and a father or uncle or somebody in high places to take care of you. It was simply the best club that ever existed - founded by the Congress of Vienna, developed by the wealth and conveniences of the industrial revolution, not yet affected by the political and social changes that have finally upset the applecart.

It was a club of charming people living a gay life in every capital from Lisbon to Istanbul. Only a few thousand families provided the personnel, so that wherever you went you met people who knew the people you knew - a truly international set in a world full of international settings, with social counterparts in every country. Ascot and Chantilly; Sandhurst and St Cyr; the Quai d'Orsay and the Wilhelmstrasse; the Bristol and the Savoy hotels in all the best places; the Merry Widow, the Charleston and the Lambeth Walk and dancing until dawn! There's magic in those words; it's remembered music that all the guns and bombs and hijackers can't destroy."

Things were easier in my time. We had then to build a service literally from scratch, and into the vacuum came tumbling a whole bunch of characters from His Majesty's exalted order of the Indian Civil Service (ICS). Members of this tribe were not available in sufficient numbers from the professions – lawyers, professors, journalists and the like. I was one of the latter.

I was thirty-seven years old when I was admitted into the Indian Foreign Service (IFS), although some years earlier, at the fag end of the war, I had been sent to Canada and then to England to head the Information Services in those countries. In between, I enjoyed junkets in Paris and Geneva for international conferences, so that I was not entirely a tyro when I was formally inducted into the service, starting off in the rank of First Secretary.

It is somewhat more difficult for today's starry-eyed aspirant. All going well – it is a stiff entrance examination – the new recruit will be given training for a year or two at headquarters in the Ministry of External Affairs, during which period he will be expected to learn (and pass) a foreign language of his choice, enjoying the title of attaché which in reality is the lowest rank in the career officer's grade. To begin with, such probationers were sent to Oxford or Cambridge (or elsewhere in Western Europe), but the economy drive under Mr Nehru's influence put an end to that practice.

It takes about fifteen years to climb the ladder, rung by rung, through Third Secretary (which the young attaché soon becomes) to First Secretary, until at last, when he is nearing forty, he should normally be approved for the selection grade as a Counsellor. As, however, such vacancies exist only in the few larger missions, some of these officers are appointed in the same grade to take charge of smaller missions or those of comparatively little importance. Thus, some lucky ones become Ambassadors or High Commissioners at the age of forty.

I was fifty when I was appointed Ambassador to Mexico, and concurrently Ambassador to Cuba and Panama. Promotions were difficult for IFS officers then because the ICS were always ahead of them and bagged all the prize posts, but I recall a Japanese Ambassador saying to me when he asked me my age: "Oh, but you are practically a baby!" Whether or not that was intended to be a compliment I never found out, but the fact was that before then I had already served as Head of Mission in two important places – Charge d'Affaires at Djakarta and Deputy High Commissioner at Lahore (our High Commissioner to Pakistan was resident at Karachi) – and in various senior capacities in a half-dozen other posts. Not such a baby therefore! The Japanese gentleman, I should add, was approaching seventy, having knocked around the globe performing numerous consular functions before attaining his present eminence.

All of which is merely a preamble to the moral of this story, which is that mere acceptance into the Foreign Service doesn't automatically make a person a diplomat. Diplomacy is a diversely defined and much-maligned word. Webster describes it as "the art and practice of conducting negotiations between nations; skill in handling affairs without arousing hostility; tact." Others are not so complimentary. One popular definition of a diplomat is that he is a man who is sent abroad to lie for the good of his country, while an unnamed Secretary of State called a new envoy "a smooth operator... a slimy son of a bitch."

*

VIP Night out

I saw service under three Ambassadors while posted to the USA. The first of these was Vijayalakshmi Pandit, and I was sorry that she left ("to re-enter politics" - she explained) about a year after my arrival. She was a remarkable person by any standard: intelligent, sensitive, quick-witted, an effective speaker and a charming hostess. She was also, like all women, capricious and utterly unpredictable.

After leading her staff a merry dance throughout a long day, Mrs. Pandit would become quite a different person during the evening. She would then curl up on the sofa in her elegant drawing-room in Washington's Cleveland Park district, slowly sip a very dry martini, and insist: "Go on, have another – don't mind me." Once after an especially tiring two days in Detroit, where she had made a number of speeches, she returned to the hotel loaded with parcels. "Whatever have you been up to?" I asked her. "I just had to take back some little souvenirs for Rowena and Aruna" she replied. They were our two daughters, aged seven and five, who delighted her by calling her "Auntie Ambassador."

One day she threw the draft of a speech I had prepared for her into my face. She made her own speeches as a rule, mostly extemporaneously, but she expected ideas to be put to her. "I can't utter such nonsense" she told me, referring to something I had written. Then when she got up to speak, she repeated every word I had suggested, and the house gave her a standing ovation. At the table with us were Adlai Stevenson, Hubert Humphrey and Walter Reuther, among other leaders of the Democratic Party. "That was a nice touch I gave" she said to me in the car while returning to the hotel, without batting an eyelid.

On another occasion, when the first American wheat shipment was being despatched to Bombay from Baltimore, I arranged that during the television shooting, a stevedore should come up to her and buss her on the cheek. "How utterly ridiculous!" she said; but when the longshoreman proceeded with the act anyway, she turned on her charm, co-operating as required. Later in the evening Marquis Childs, the columnist, said to her: "You know, Nan, you could make a fortune in Hollywood." She didn't take this seriously, but beamed at me as if she had thought the whole thing herself.

One morning she buzzed me on the intercom. "Come over" she said, I walked from my office to hers three rooms away, and she said to me: "There's this gentleman who requires special treatment." She mentioned the name of a visiting senior politician (who was expected to be taken into the Cabinet), who I shall call Lalaji. "He is staying at the Shoreham Hotel" she told me, "and wants to see the night life of the capital. Do the best you can, but be very careful. I don't have to tell you that he is a Very Important Person."

When I got to his hotel room in the evening Lalaji was still in his dhoti and Jawahar jacket, a white khadi cap perched jauntily on his balding pate. I asked him what he would like to do. He scratched himself under his dhoti and said to me: "First of all I want you to give me a typical American meal. The very thing that all the natives eat. Then I want you to take me to one of those night spots where I believe that half-naked women perform. I must take back with me a correct impression so that I may brief our people correctly."

I suggested to him that he should perhaps dress a little more appropriately, whereupon he changed into a black serge coat, buttoned up at the collar, and baggy trousers to match. He kept the khadi cap on his head. "Is this all right?" he asked when he emerged from the bathroom half an hour later, and when I insisted that he should remove the cap as it made him look conspicuous, he gave me a nasty look and transferred the headpiece into one of his pockets.

First I took him to a nearby Hotte Shoppe, which restaurants are (or were) a distinguishing feature of the Washington scene. "This is where the average American eats" I told him. He saw a sign advertising "Cheeseburgers" and insisted that he would have one of those, with a milk-shake on the side, seeing others partaking of the same meal at adjoining tables. He polished off the first beef patty and the accompanying dill pickles, and then asked for another. I had been told that he was a vegetarian, but who was I to object to his pleasure?

He rubbed his stomach gleefully. "Now to hit the town" he said, using an expression he must have picked up from the movies. "I'd like to tell our people how the great American public spends its evenings."

Washington wasn't much of a place for nightclubs in those days, but there were one or two sleazy joints I had come to know in the course of my duties. So I took him to "Sloppy Joe's" where I was lucky to find a corner table in the smoke-filled basement room, and I said to him: "I hope you're not a teetotaller, sir. I'll have to order a drink for you and they don't serve Coca-Colas here."

He giggled. Already he had noticed the bare-bosomed lady gyrating on the small revolving stage, and this had perked him up. "Well," he said, "as they say, when in Rome do as the Romans do. Yes, I'll have a whisky, but make mine a Scotch, not that horrible bourbon, if you don't mind."

Before our order arrived, a cigarette girl came up to our table and I bought a packet of Chesterfields from her. Lalaji kept staring at her long, net-stockinged legs with goggle eyes, but reprimanded me when he saw the dollar tip I gave her. "That's how you young fellows waste your money", he commented.

He asked for another drink, and then another, and put these back as if to the manner born. When one of the hostesses came and sat at our table, he asked the busty blonde to dance with him. He wasn't a particularly skilful dancer, but in the crush of the tiny floor, it hardly made a difference. Only I could observe one of his hands slipping down to her ample rear.

He bought her back to the table. "This nice girl's name is Dolores" he told me. "She wants to come back to the hotel with me for a drink." When she went to fetch her wrap, I turned upon Lalalji. "Do you know," I asked him, "that that woman's a professional whore? She carries more sickness on her than the infectious diseases wing of a hospital. The people at the Shoreham will recognise her immediately. Lalaji, this kind of thing has been the undoing of many a good and innocent man. We must get rid of her, but fast. Leave everything to me."

He looked at me penitently. "Whatever you say", he said meekly, and when Dolores returned I thrust a ten-dollar bill inside her cleavage and told her that my friend had been taken ill. Half an hour later Lalaji was in his hotel bed, snoring away like a contended babe.

In the morning I went to report to the Ambassador. Lalaji was already there, khadi cap and all. "Ah, my good friend of last night", he said gushingly. "Madame", he added, turning to the Ambassador, "you have a great diplomat here." She looked up from her file and gave me a smile.

*

'Till the end of time

"Praise not the day until evening has come", says a Scandinavian proverb, "nor a sword until it is tried, nor a maiden until she is wed". Our grandmothers put it differently. "The proof of the pudding is in the eating", they said, or "Time enough to proffer thanks after you have finished the curry."

I could relate a dozen stories to illustrate this adage, or to debunk it; but I want to tell about Ali Akbar Khan and his friendship for me. We were at school together in Ferozepore when we first swore eternal fealty, and then at Government College, Lahore, and bumped into each other every so often after both of us had graduated. Then came the partition; and we found ourselves on different sides of the fence.

Even in the old days I recall that Akbar was the soul of caution. He would bang every rupee on the counter to see if the ring was true and prod every mango and bring it to his nose to ensure that the quality was right. "One can't afford to be careless", he was fond of saying, and, "Once bitten, twice shy."

I was pleasantly surprised to find that he was First Secretary at the Pakistan Embassy at Djakarta when I arrived in the Indonesian capital in 1955, just a few days before the start of the Bandung Conference.[1] Already the two of us were veterans of the Foreign Service, in a manner of speaking: While I had done duty in Canada, the U.K., Holland and the U.S.A., he had been in Japan and the Philippines. I remember saying to myself at the time how much smarter their people in Karachi were by letting their chaps specialize in a certain region. We, on the other hand, plucked our man from an environment with which he had just become familiar and sent him thousands or miles away, thence to be shunted off again just when he was beginning to feel his way around properly.

Relations between our two countries were not particularly pally in those days, and Akbar took a considerable risk by coming out to the airport to greet me, ostensibly to collect the diplomatic bag, which chore is usually performed by an Assistant or a Section Officer. Suddenly he appeared from inside a telephone booth, feigned a look of surprise, and shouted for all to hear: "Fancy meeting you here!" Then, without further ado, he crushed me in a bear hug - he was twice my size and when I say "crushed" I mean crushed. Later he explained: "I've got to be careful. The old man's a bit of a diehard. Although he comes from Lucknow originally, there's an overdose of poison in his system. But I suppose you have blokes like that in your own service."

India played a major role at Bandung. As anyone will agree, the principal figures there were our own Nehru, Chou En-lai of China, Nasser of Egypt, Tito of Yugoslavia and, of course, Sukarno of Indonesia. These were non-alignment's "big five", and although all five have now gone, the developing world still remembers their

---

[1] Bandung Conference (1955) was organised by Indonesia, Burma, Pakistan, Ceylon (Sri Lanka) and India. The aim was to promote Afro-Asian economic and cultural cooperation and to oppose US and Soviet colonialism in the setting of cold war tensions.

unique contribution to a movement that has become a recognised force in global politics.

Neither Akbar nor I had personally anything to do at Bandung itself. We were "holding the fort" in our offices in the capital, glorified head clerks keeping the files moving while our chiefs were huddled with the Prime Ministers in the cool of Java's main hill resort. However, we both put on grand airs, and it was amusing to see how we were wooed by the Western missions who did their damnedest to pump something out of us. Akbar's position was not entirely merited, as Pakistan had hardly anything to do at the conference, but the British treated him as if he were Liaquat Ali Khan[2] himself and Akbar didn't mind a bit!

But back to my story.

Another pleasure was to find that my friend had been bitten by the golf bug. He played as atrociously as myself - but what fun we had on the links beyond the kampongs, close to the harbour at Tandjung Priok! It all began somewhat surreptitiously – "I've got to be careful, you know" - but in due course Akbar got his Ambassador to agree that it might not be such a bad thing if we were to be seen knocking the wee white ball around in open view of our other colleagues - few others but diplomats played golf in the Djakarta of those days.

We were sitting outside the little clubhouse one evening, foaming tankards of Amstel lager on the table in front of us - despite their hatred for the Dutch, Indonesians prefer the beer of Holland. At another table an Anglo-Saxon foursome stared at us as if in disbelief, until one of them remembered his manners and yelled across the distance: "Hi there! Warm evening, eh?"

Although dead beat after 24 holes in the afternoon sun, I was in a jubilant mood. For the first time I had gone round the course in ninety strokes and, although I had won our regular bet, I told Akbar in a mood of magnanimity that the drinks were on me. He eyed me suspiciously. "Those chaps at that table will think that you've gone soft in the head. They'd much rather see the two of us at each other's throats."

He took a hefty swig and added: "Why don't people realise that hatred isn't a permanent emotion, that because circumstances

---

[2] 1st Prime Minister of Pakistan.

compelled our two people to separate, it doesn't mean that we should be going hammer and tongs all the time? With my hand on my heart I say to you that I have no ill feeling for India – I'll go so far as to say that I love your people as much as I love mine. How, in any case, could a political operation alter the affection that we two, for example, have nurtured for each other since our childhood days?"

I have always been a sucker for sentimental talk, especially when those much bandied words, friendship and loyalty, are brought into play. It was in such a moment of weakness that I inched my chair closer to his, "Akbar", I said. "I have a problem. I don't know if you can help me, but I'd like to mention it to you. If nothing else, at least I will have got it off my chest."

We have in Indonesia, as in other South-East Asian countries and elsewhere, a considerable Indian community. They are a mixed lot, most of them having settled there before the convulsion that shook our sub-continent in 1947. The bulk of them are prosperous and well-to-do, but some are downright poor. By and large, they are well integrated and on good terms with the local population and members of their own society. But, as in every pond, there are some bad fish, and it is these who cause the most headaches to Embassy officials.

I told Akbar about Abdul Rashid, who had come out from Amritsar in the late forties. He had started off with a small cloth retail shop in the main bazaar and had immediately struck oil. Now he had branches in Medan and Sourabaya, and recently had brought out a master tailor from Calcutta to meet the demands of his growing, sophisticated clientele, including (it was said) the President of the Republic.

Willy-nilly, Abdul Rashid had become the leader of the local Indian Muslims, but we had received reports that he was inciting them by spreading allegations of persecution of the minority communities by the Government of India and all manner of rash stories about the Indian role in Kashmir. Besides, through a recent Singapore connection, he was violating the exchange regulations by transferring a large portion of his profits abroad. Within the limits of discretion, I had tried to dissuade him, but to no avail.

I told Akbar: "I'd like you to reason with him, if you can. Tell him that the larger interests of our two countries demand harmony and cooperation rather than suspicion and discord. Personally, I see a time when we will have a relationship similar to that between the USA. and

Canada, but this will be easier to achieve if our two peoples at least refrain from loose talk. Abdul Rashid will listen to you. He is profoundly religious, and perhaps you could tackle him one day after the Friday prayers."

Akbar nodded his head, finished his beer, and we talked of other things. Some months later I heard that he was being recalled to Karachi. I telephoned him at his office and we agreed to meet at the Hotel des Indes in the evening. "I'm in disgrace", he told me. "That Abdul Rashid of yours went and reported me to my Ambassador. The long and short of it is that I am suspect and not to be trusted any more. I'm being sent back to headquarters, and leave next week. After that, Allah knows what will happen!"

I myself was transferred to Pakistan - to Lahore - after my stint in Indonesia. On my periodical visits to Karachi, whenever I asked about Akbar Ali Khan, I was given evasive replies. Years later, I learned that he had joined the family business in Pauralpindi. We never met again; but whenever people talk of proof of friendship, I think of him, and I feel sad and lonely.

*

At the summit

It was Dale Carnegie, I believe, who recommended to aspirants that, among other things, they should develop the knack of attracting attention. If, therefore, conspicuousness is one of the ingredients of success, then our delegates at international conferences are usually several steps up the ladder.

My first experience of what might be called a summit meeting was the Peace Conference held at the Palais du Luxembourg in the autumn of 1946. Still a greenhorn and new to affairs of state, I had barely settled into my new post in Canada when out of the blue, one fine morning, I received instructions asking me to join our delegation in Paris. You could have knocked me down with a feather; but twenty-four hours later I was winging across the Atlantic in an RCAF[3]

---

[3] Royal Canadian Air Force

transport plane. After an overnight stop in London, an official car was speeding me from Orly airport to the Hotel Royal Monceau, where Indian delegations used to be lodged, and probably still are.

Next day I was rubbing shoulders with Molotov and Vyshinsky, Byrnes and Bevin, General Smuts and Ho Chi Minh, and a gentleman named Lee Bum Suk. Rubbing shoulders is perhaps an exaggeration, but I felt important enough just being in the same room and breathing the same air as men who had walked the stage of history.

None of these notables would have attracted a second glance had he walked down the street incognito - Smuts maybe, if he happened to be wearing his field marshal's uniform, ribbons and all; otherwise they would have just been lost in the crowd. Individually, they had arresting features, but certainly no photographer would have chosen any of them to pose for a portrait advertising a Man of Distinction.

This honour belonged to one of our very own. He had a name as long as that of a Spanish grandee, to which a variety of British titles were liberally appended, but his friends knew him simply as Gopi. I recall how giggling teenagers would jostle each other when, somewhat later than the others, he would arrive, shining black locks curling below a turban which would have shamed a cockatoo, and swagger past rows of the Garde Republicaine in the manner of a cavalry officer to find his way into the marble-columned grand salon of the Palais.

Paris in those days was not the glittering place it is today, or had been some years earlier. It had been spared the physical ravages of war suffered by capitals such as London and Berlin, for example, although it had had its full share of suffering and privation. Its citizens were sullen and suspicious of the foreigner, resentful of those more affluent than themselves, afraid and unforthcoming.

But no one was afraid of Gopi, and he would flash an indulgent smile while scrawling his autograph on copy-books and newspapers or any handy piece of paper pushed under his nose. He never made a speech throughout the conference, but contributed to the more ponderous of its deliberations by drafting speeches here and there. He was easily the most popular foreign visitor in the French capital at that time. He was generous to a fault.

The Krishna Menons and Jam Sahebs were to appear on the scene in later years. And others noted for their wit or wealth or other diverse talents; such as the Cabinet Minister from New Delhi who arrived for breakfast in the dining-room of Geneva's Hotel Beau Rivage attired in pink striped pyjamas. Or the secretary-general of one of our delegations who discovered on arising from his slumber that his nocturnal companion had decamped not only with his new Leica camera and Grundig transistor, but also the packet containing the delegates' weekly allowance and the salaries of the local staff. Or another pillar of our community, who insisted on sampling the eating places and other night spots of an African capital - only hours after we had suffered a national tragedy. A book could be written about such people, and probably will, but the Malik Sahib stood apart from them: a man of rare charm who could not harm anyone by word or deed and who conducted himself with certain flair, an *élan* which his successors might do well to emulate.

There is another conference coterie, a second echelon, so to speak - the Advisers, made up of middle-ranking civil servants and the like - the members of which regard themselves, with some justification, as no less important than the panjandrums who adorn the front chairs of a summit meeting. They are the backroom boys, the backbone of all conferences, those who slog away all day and try, as one of them once said: "to make hay - hay after the sun stops shining."

A small group such as this one was seated around a table at one of our favourite restaurants, the Teheran I believe it is still called, a mere stone's throw from the Arc de Triomphe, where there was always rice on the menu and never a shortage of yoghurt; important considerations for representatives of a secular state. It was our custom to go Dutch on such occasions, the senior member of our party playing host and collecting the damages later. This evening even the vegetarians had consumed somewhat more than their normal ration of vin ordinaire, but a hard day's work was out of the way and the night was young.

"Garçon!" called Gopi, our host of the evening. He had picked up a smattering of the language and showed it off whenever he could. "Garçon," he demanded, "L'addition, s'il vous plait," and no matter that this sounded to some of us as if he wanted to work out an equation on a silver plate.

The conference was drawing to a close, and we had had a little free time of our own. As I said, the night was young; so we passed a unanimous vote and decided to "do" the town. Gopi looked into a little red diary, and moments later we had crammed into a delegation car and were making for the Left Bank. Soon we were in a smoke-filled bistro where men dressed as women were dancing with fierce-looking characters wearing black berets, sideburns touching their chins and cigarettes dangling from their lips. Bare-breasted girls were serving a motley crew of other customers. Nowadays such a sight might not cause a lama to raise an eyebrow, but this was before today's permissive society and I confess we were a little fidgety, to say the least. Suddenly Gopi was consulting his notebook. "Allons!" he commanded, and then with a fresh burst of hidden versatility, "Tempus fugit!"

We piled into the little Citroen once again and re-crossed the Seine. In the shadow of the Sacre Coeur, Gopi led us on a conducted tour of various establishments immortalized on canvas and in book and song. The good Lord only knows how much champagne and how many cognacs later we agreed, now that our pockets were empty, to head for home.

The concierge yawned his disapproval and the chambermaids looked up from their scrubbing when we stole into our rooms. Somewhere a cock crowed. At the stroke of nine, however, we were at our appointed places for the daily delegation meeting. Gopi had already deposited on the Leader's pad a neatly typed draft of a speech which our representative was to deliver in the political committee, something about the treatment of persons of Indian origin in South Africa. Gopi hadn't slept a wink that night, but he looked fresh as a daisy, and if anyone suspected his nocturnal shenanigans, this was concealed as carefully as a state secret.

"I call on the distinguished Representative of India," said the Committee Chairman, and our chief delegate put on his reading glasses, adjusted his khadi cap, fingered the pink rose in his achkan and proceeded to read word for word the draft Gopi had so carefully prepared. After forty minutes there was a round of applause. The resolution was put to the vote. And Victory!

Outside the conference cafeteria, a beaming chief delegate cornered our friend. "It went down well, didn't it?" he asked Gopi, but this was a statement more than a question. "Best speech I ever made. After all, it's the speaker's personality and manner of delivery that wins a case, don't you think?"

Humbly, Gopi bowed his head and murmured his acquiescence.

The return of the Buddha

It wasn't much of a treasure, really. I'd picked up the bronze Buddha for a few rupees from a Tibetan's stall on Queensway before the GI's arrived to spoil the market for everyone. I then got into the habit of rubbing its plump little belly every morning before setting out for work, and I believed that this brought me good luck. Now my wife had gone and given it away to Greta Golden. I was furious.

We first met Greta at a cocktail party in Toronto in the winter following the end of World War II. We'd just arrived from India, and the party was in our honour. She was wearing a vivid crimson sari, tied in a style peculiar to Western women, and she had a black mark in the middle of her forehead. Her skin was like parchment and her hair was streaked with grey, but it was clear that she had been a beauty in her time. She still had the figure of a film star, aided of course by those various contraptions in which American garment manufacturers seem to specialize.

Unlike today, when most foreign cities are bursting at the seams with immigrants, there were hardly any Indians in the Ontarian capital then. So far as I can remember, apart from my wife and myself and our infant daughter, the only others were the Trade Commissioner and his family of seven; his clerk-of-all-work, a clean-shaven Sikh named Jerry Hundal, whose forebears had come out as indentured labourers at the turn of the century to help build the Canadian Pacific Railroad; and a petty trader named Ram something or other who owned a store just off Yonge Street, where he stocked pickles and condiments and odds and ends like brass bells and handloom tablecloths. How he made a living was a mystery, as Indian goods weren't much known and even less in demand.

When we were introduced to her, Greta Golden folded her hands in the authentic manner and muttered a low "Namaste". Then she stuck to us, not letting go until we had agreed to have supper with her on the following Saturday. "Just a small get-together", she confided. "Intimate. A few personal friends to greet you lovely people from across the seven seas", and she laughed a husky, come-hither laugh. Yes, she must have been a most attractive young lady.

At her place she had on a black sari, but the mark on her forehead was vermilion, and all manner of coloured beads hung from her neck and tinkled around her wrists. Her small apartment was thick with incense smoke, despite which the rooms smelled of curry powder. "Ram brought me these agarbattis",[4] she explained. "They come from Mysore. Isn't the fragrance heavenly? But come, I should take you around."

There was a dentist and his wife, someone from the U.S. Consulate, two spinsters who gave ballet lessons, a reporter from the Globe & Mail, and the ubiquitous Mr. Ram. They discussed Gandhi and the non-co-operation movement, berated Churchill as "an old diehard" and Wavell for "dilatory tactics", and praised the valour of Indian troops in the Western Desert. Then Greta beat a little brass gong to announce that dinner was ready.

The less said about the curry the better, but the salad was delicious. The Canadians - all North Americans, in fact - are wonderful with cucumbers and lettuce and tomatoes; they add walnuts and a half-dozen other ingredients, top this with what they call a Seven Islands dressing, and it becomes a meal fit for a king. However, the other guests preferred the Indian-style food, and the dentist's wife smacked her lips as she went for her third helping and said: "Love that sauce on the mutton, Greta darling - mmm, out of this world! You must let me have the recipe." Later, as everyone was leaving, Greta took my wife aside and gave her a small flat parcel, which we later discovered to be an atlas of North America with an encyclopaedic supplement - an appropriate gift by any reckoning.

A month or so later we gave our first party. We hadn't found a place of our own yet and were still living in the Alexandra Palace Hotel on University Avenue, where entertaining was expensive. But this was my first foreign assignment and I was in a hurry. A whole world lay spread out at my feet, waiting to be conquered. Besides, we already owed many lunches and dinners. One of the qualifications of a diplomat is that he should display good manners, and the lowest form of boorishness is not to reciprocate in matters like receiving presents

---

[4] Indian incense.

and accepting hospitality. My job, as I saw it, was to make friends and influence people. What better way than to throw a party?

It wasn't such a big affair, about thirty people altogether, but it was distinguished by the presence of Mayor Robert L. Saunders, who wanted to show his appreciation of the fact that some days earlier at short notice, I had filled in for another speaker to address the monthly meeting off the Commonwealth Club, of which he was that year's President. Greta was there, of course, dressed this time in a green shot-silk Benares sari, and she was the last to leave. She seemed to think that she had some kind of proprietary interest in the party, having sent us a carton of assorted canapés, "to help you folks out", as the note the delivery man gave us said.

After she had kissed both of us on the cheeks and said goodnight and as she was making for the door, on the spur of the moment my wife picked up the little bronze Buddha we kept perched on the mantelpiece and pressed it into her hands. "For being such a good friend", she whispered into her ear. Greta had admired the statuette when she came to call on us for the first time, praising it to the skies and begging us to find a replica. Now she was overwhelmed by the suddenness of the presentation.

As I said, I was furious, but there was nothing I could do about it now. I sulked for a day or two, and then forgot all about the figurine. Statues come and statues go, but life must continue, earnest, inexorable.

We continued to see Greta Golden off and on, but then in September of the following year, just after India achieved independence, I received orders transferring me to London. Greta wrote to us once or twice, and when we got moved again, this correspondence became restricted to a card at Christmas. In due course it fell off entirely, and when the time came for us to come home to roost, I am ashamed to admit that we had half-forgotten our Canadian friend altogether.

Then, one day I was surprised to receive in the post a parcel stamped with the seal of the Ministry of External Affairs - surprised, because the mandarins over there have little time for old has-beens. The cover contained another package with a Toronto postmark, and inside this was my Buddha and a letter from Mr Ram, who was now (according to the letterhead) the proprietor of the "City's Most Exclusive Specialty Store", and in it he informed us that Greta

Golden had died in the previous month. "Before she died," he wrote, "she asked me to return to you the Buddha you gave her and to tell you how much solace it gave her in her last days. She knew how attached you were to the statuette, and this is the reason why she wished to restore it to your possession."

The Learned One now sits cross-legged on the shelf facing the desk on which I write. His eyes are closed and on his face is an aura of fulfilment and tranquillity. A smile seems to hover around his lips, and yet I detect a hint of sadness as if reflecting on the follies of man and the perils that stalk his troubled world.

*

Portrait of a gentleman

I was fortunate early in my career to serve under so good a man that it became a wrench when the time came for me to take his leave. Although it is doubtful that he will see these lines, I have altered his name in the further hope that, should he happen to do so, he will not recognise himself, as otherwise it might cause him some distress. He was a person who shunned personal publicity of any kind, one of those who believed that, if there is any merit in one's actions: that should be its own reward.

Dr. Madan Mohan and I had newly arrived to open an embassy in a Western European capital and neither of us, nor the four or five other functionaries who came from India with us, had much experience of formal diplomatic life and the various demands it makes on the incumbent. There were, of course, reference books one could look up and veterans in other missions one could consult, but nevertheless the novelty of it all was both exciting and a little frightening.

He was a bachelor, a vegetarian and a teetotaller - not exactly an easy combination for one about to make his debut as an ambassador. This was off set to some extent by the circumstance that his second-in-command (myself) was none of these. My wife and two small children were due to join me shortly; we ate fish, fowl and filet mignon with equal gusto; and I could drink a lord under the table - and sometimes did.

We had been put up in a former castle, now converted into a luxury hotel. Situated in a forest on the outskirts of the capital, it had served as a Nazi headquarters during the Occupation, and when we arrived for dinner on the first evening we were introduced to the major domo, an extroverted type named Nicholas ("Call me Niko").

I took Niko aside and carefully explained to him that His Excellency from India was a strict vegetarian, which meant that meat or meat preparations of any kind were abhorrent to him. Because there are so many misconceptions on the subject, I added that it was not so much a matter of religion as a way of life, the result of upbringing and habit. The maitre d' listened with rapt attention, his steel grey eyes piercing mine, then nodded in comprehension and assured me that I should have no cause for the slightest anxiety. Thereupon I ordered the table d'hote for myself and a potage and various salads etc., for my boss.

Imagine my horror, therefore, when with the first course I noticed an entire giblet floating in the Ambassador's soup. I summoned Niko and reproved him, suggesting that perhaps he had not understood me. The poor man was a picture of abject misery. "But, mynheer," he replied, his face red as a beetroot, "I understood perfectly. With my own eyes I supervised the chef when he strained the soup!"

Dr. Mohan was equal to the occasion. With superb aplomb, he removed the offending piece of flesh with a fork and placed it aside. "Accidents will happen," he said, flashing his most winning smile, and continued with his meal as if nothing had happened.

This was a weekend, and the following Tuesday the Lord Chamberlain arrived to escort the Ambassador-designate to the palace in the old capital, forty miles away, where the Queen was in residence. An hour earlier the Chief of Protocol had rehearsed with us, with that meticulous precision which is the hallmark of such ceremonies in every monarchy, the formalities for the presentation of credentials. Both men stood over six feet tall and were decked out in uniforms which must have been designed for a field marshal - buckles and bows and gold braid and decorations in every colour of the rainbow. Then Dr. Mohan made his appearance. Ramrod straight, he matched them inch for inch, and in his simple black achkan, white churidars and Khadi cap, he looked like an emperor. And when he inspected the hussars lined up outside the palace, a cheer went up from the crowd which had been attracted by the trooping of the guard. The Queen herself had done him an unusual honour by receiving him so soon after his arrival, and she underscored this by detaining him for longer than the time prescribed by the regulations. They became good friends.

Some days later the diplomatic corps were asked to attend a function to commemorate the country's war dead. We had just taken our places in front of a tall obelisk when the clouds opened up and the rain came down in the manner of a monsoon shower. Our other colleagues, more experienced in this and other matters, had come better prepared: their formal clothes cleverly concealed by waterproof materials. But poor Dr. Mohan! A limp achkan clung to his lean frame, and what remained on his head resembled a skull cap. I whispered to him that I would find an umbrella or some other protective covering, but he gave me a stern look, and when he went forward to lay his wreath, he resembled someone who had been dragged out of a pond. Both of us were sneezing when we returned to the residence, and shortly afterwards a courier arrived from the palace with a letter from the Queen admonishing the Ambassador for not taking proper precautions against "our abominable weather" and recommending a certain potion as a panacea for chills and bronchial complaints.

It was a small mission as missions go, but a busy one, not so much because of the amount of work we handled as for the zeal with which all of us went about our business. He had inspired this in us. He was a devout Gandhian. We learnt anew from his example the significance of truth and simplicity and the importance of means in accomplishing ends. He had also acquired a rich repertoire of saws of the Western world. "Hard work never killed anybody" was one of his favourites. And: "One good turn deserves another".

During this time a round-table conference was held between representatives of the host country and of their former colonial empire. We had nothing to do with this, of course, but Dr. Mohan offered his good offices, and these were accepted with alacrity. Consequently, from early morning till late at night we were liaising between both sides, rushing hither and thither, offering drafts, transmitting cables and attempting conciliation and moderation when conflict and breakdown appeared possible. Every member of the staff wanted to make a contribution which might relieve the burden and anxiety of the Ambassador and, although our popularity zoomed, all of us were worn to a frazzle.

After about a year or so Dr. Mohan took a brief holiday and visited the Swiss Alps. On the day of his return, he came straight to the Chancery and sent for me.

"Yes, Sir?"

"Sit down. I'll be with you in a moment."

He finished with the file he was reading, moved into an easy chair and said he wanted to tell me about his trip. He spoke of the mountain air and the trees and the flowers, but suddenly he assumed a serious mien, "I did something very foolish, too," he said sadly, "and don't know how to tell about it." He hesitated for a while, as if attempting to frame the right words, and then shrugged his shoulders. "Ah, well, there's no fool like an old fool, as they say."

Beneath his newly acquired tan he looked pale, and all manner of horrible thoughts went through my mind. Had this dear, simple man been seduced by one of those post-war butterflies who frequented the fashionable holiday resorts and watering places, and was he being held for blackmail? He played an occasional game of bridge - had an international shark done him out of an impossible sum of money? Or had he helped someone in distress who was an impostor? I decided there and then that, whatever he had done, I would bail him out, even if it meant offering myself as a scapegoat.

My fears were short-lived, however. "I took skiing lessons," he confessed at last. "Imagine – I'll never see fifty again, and there I was on those slopes, turning and twisting and comporting myself amongst teenagers and people half my years. I wonder what they'd have done back in Delhi if I'd broken a leg or something - fired me I suppose?"

That question was soon answered, for he did fall down and break a leg while ice-skating on a frozen waterway. During his convalescence he sent me a note, and with it was a cheque. "I want you to make plans to take a holiday, a long week-end or some such thing," he wrote, "effective the very day I get out of this wretched bed. I know how heavily you have been pressed, and I know too that such holidays are expensive. The enclosed slip of paper will help a little. I hope you will make use of it in the same spirit that I send it to you - the gratitude of a cantankerous old fogey."

I was transferred a few weeks later and could never make use of that 'slip of paper', which still reposes in my portfolio of mementoes. Dr. Mohan came to see us off on to the Channel steamer which was to take us first to England, and then in one of the *Queens* to the USA He embraced my wife, kissed our children and shook my hand. One of our friends from another mission, who also came to say goodbye, remarked: "You'll never see the likes of him again."

I never did.

*

2

How not to be a diplomat

Let me present a rogue's gallery of travelling showmen.

Atma Ram was in one of the first batches to appear before the Selection Board in those early days. He was bright as a newly-minted rupee and was looked upon as the man most likely to get to the very top. One of the smart things he did was to marry the daughter of a Secretary to one of The Ministries, which opened to him every door in the South and North Blocks right through the Establishment. He had been recruited straight out of the army and had the swagger and accent (and moustache) of a cavalry officer. Immediately we nicknamed him "Sandy" – for Sandhurst – which sobriquet he loved.

His first posting was to an East European country badly impoverished by the war – indeed, which country in Europe, apart from a few such as Switzerland and Sweden, was not similarly impoverished and rendered down-at-heel? Soon, in his new environment, he was cultivating members of the former aristocracy, in tatters now and poor as church mice but holding on to possessions which might once have been priceless but now could hardly buy a pound of butter or a tin of baby food. Bit by bit, in exchange for such hard-to-get commodities, Sandy picked up an oil painting here, a Bokhara rug there, adding to these acquisitions fine sets of silver, crystal and porcelain tableware, plus diverse other knick-knacks. In terms of today's prices, he amassed a king's treasure.

Thus Atma Ram had acquired quite a collection when, some two years later, he was transferred to the Consulate-General in New York. Here he set himself up modestly to begin with, but as his little apartment began to burst at the seams with his European loot, he was compelled to move to a place with an extra bedroom and more storage space. Then opportunity knocked again in the person of a visiting potentate, who brought with him a letter from his father-in-law enjoining him to "Render such assistance as you can for this good friend." Ostensibly the former Maharaja had come for medical treatment, for which purposes he had been sanctioned a liberal amount of scarce foreign exchange.

Atma Ram rendered the visitor the best of available assistance, so much so that he and his wife were invited to share the visiting gentleman's penthouse apartment on Fifth Avenue, which anyway was much too large for a single person and was vacant for much of the time as the tenant was constantly travelling. Sandy's wife became one of the big city's most popular hostesses, her pictures appearing in *Good Housekeeping* and other glossy magazines. Whenever His Highness entertained in his lavish style, it was the young couple who received the encomiums.

I was having a drink with them in this new residence one evening when Atma Ram, in an expansive moment, confided to me that he continued to draw his official rental allowance although he now lived in accommodation that was costing him nothing. I asked him how he could reconcile this, apart from the Accountant-General Central Revenues, with his own conscience. He was quite unabashed. "Machiavelli says" he replied, "that in diplomacy what matters most is how one plays one's cards. I'm only doing the best I can with what the pack has dealt me." I wanted to tell him that Machiavelli also said that a diplomat was meant to be a gentleman and that honesty and integrity came first on a gentleman's list of priorities. But what the heck, I told myself, it had nothing to do with me.

Nobody was surprised when Atma Ram, before any of us, was promoted Counsellor and given comfortable berth in London, where too he found ways to make hay, rain or shine. Then he was transferred to the Ministry and promoted to become Chief of Protocol, which job he performed as if to the manner born. Meanwhile, he had sold, for a tidy little profit, two automobiles he had imported duty-free, plus other items like air-conditioners, refrigerators, etc, from the proceeds of which he started building a house on the plot he had been allocated in New Delhi's Defence Colony. The rules were lax in those days, and people like our friend Sandy literally got away with murder.

Then followed a succession of ambassadorial assignments, in each of which Atma Ram acquitted himself with his usual distinction, managing at the same time to stockpile and send back an assortment of gadgetry and furnishings for what was to become his final residence. Glowing reports were sent from these posts to the Ministry. In one of these, they described how he had succeeded, at great personal effort and expense, in persuading the local Government to shift its support from Pakistan to our candidate for vacancies in the United Nations and its specialised agencies, and how he had weaned the large mercantile community from trading with China, with which country our relations were then unfriendly, to put it mildly. He forgot to mention that the President of the State to which he was accredited was a fanatical admirer of Gandhi and Nehru and all things Indian and would go out of his way to support any of our policies; further, that our merchant's trade with China had been non-existent, anyway.

Eventually, as must all of us, Atma Ram retired from the service and is now settled, very nicely thank you, in "Sandy's Repose", the house he built for himself in the Defence Colony. Old Masters adorn the walls of the drawing-room and all the bedrooms are air-conditioned. Inflation has hit him too, but he still manages to live in the style to which he has always been accustomed. When people speak of him, they describe his meteoric career and refer to him as a model diplomat. He agrees entirely.

*

Gather ye rosebuds

Diplomacy, like any other profession, spawns its own impostors. Here today, gone tomorrow, they bring the charm of novelty to what can be an otherwise humdrum existence. One of these was Jeremy Jackson, and a kinder, wittier, more charming and more beguiling character I have yet to meet.

He was the British Embassy's "India Expert", which designation took in the other members of the sub-continent, and he occupied a cabin next to the office of the Counsellor for Political Affairs. Why they wanted such a specialist in Mexico - a country so far removed from matters of Commonwealth concern I never discovered, but the fact remained that, although he wasn't listed in the "Book" (being what is known as a "local recruit"), he was far and away the most popular individual in the diplomatic colony. A bachelor, he was especially in demand by the unattached ladies of the foreign community.

We first met at a party given by the Canadian Ambassador. There were forty of us altogether and after dinner someone asked: "Anyone care to make a bridge four?" I never say no to such an invitation, and that is how I found myself at the same table with Jeremy Jackson. By some strange coincidence, although we cut after each rubber, he was not my partner throughout the long evening.

The stakes were high – a dollar a point – and, in keeping with the general atmosphere, all of us were a little merry as well. My Canadian colleague was a connoisseur so far as vintages, etc., are concerned, and I must say we did his hospitality full justice. The bidding, therefore, was somewhat on the bold side, and when the game ended I found myself ninety points down the drain.

Fiddling in my pockets, I found to my dismay that I had left both wallet and cheque-book behind, but Jeremy came to the rescue. "Not to worry, old chap" he said. "Your credit should be as good as anyone's in this room. Send me the damages whenever you feel like it." And then he asked if I would be so kind as to give him a lift home as his own "jalopy" was hors de combat.

It wasn't a long drive, but in those fifteen or twenty minutes he gave me a resume of his background, somewhat in the manner of an artist sketching an outline with deft, bold strokes of the pencil. "When I was with Mountbatten" he began, and went on to describe how he had met Mahatma Gandhi, as well as Nerhu, Jinnah, Patel, "and all the top brass." He said: "What a heady time it was – like a bottle of Dom Perignon bubbling over."

I asked him how he happened to be in Delhi at this critical period in India's history. "I was Dickie's aide in SEAC"[5] he told me. "When old Attlee wanted him to take over as Viceroy, he insisted that I should come along. Simple as pie, old chap." He added that, earlier, he had

---

[5] South East Asia Command. The body set up in charge of Allied operations in the South-East Asian Theatre of World War II.

been one of the last to come out of Dunkirk and that he had been with Monty's Desert Rats when the Eighth Army "Hit Rommel and his Panzers for six." His father had been a colonel in "Poonah", he went on, but his parents had sent him to "old Blighty" when he was still a boy, and after Eton and Oxford, he found a gaping void staring him in the face. "That's when Corporal Hitler came along and some of us got a new lease of life. For some poor buggers it was the end, of course."

After his time in India, he had drifted hither and thither, looking for the right ambience, the proper milieu. Here in Latin America he had found it. The pace was slower and the people were easy-going. "Rushing's not too good for the old ticker – wouldn't you say, old chap?"

A week or two later my wife and children arrived, and Jeremy became a regular visitor to our home. I have noted that he was a bachelor; he was handsome to boot, and his steel-grey hair and trim figure put people in mind of Cary Grant. He ran about in a cherry-red Jaguar and had a "pad" in one of the exclusive residential districts. He excelled in all sports; but his true genius was at the card table – bridge, poker, rummy, you name it, he played it, and always won, which perhaps answered the general question: "Where does he get all that money from?" After all, a local recruit is not that highly paid and he doesn't in normal circumstances have diplomatic privileges, although the Head of Mission can, at his discretion, provide him with whiskey and cigarettes on occasion.

Our two daughters had just sprouted into their teens, and they fell for Jeremy hook, line and sinker, no matter that there was a difference of more than thirty years between their ages. Soon he graduated from "Uncle Jerry" to "Jerry" and when they found that he was crazy over curry and Indian food, they developed a sudden interest in the kitchen. They pampered him with burnt and indigestible pakodas and suchlike, but Jerry took all this in good humour.

When Jawahalal Nehru was due on a State visit, Jeremy begged that I should arrange for him to meet the Prime Minister. This I did, at breakfast in the Presidential suite atop the hotel where he was accommodated, and I also squeezed in one or two other close friends who did not qualify by protocol to meet the great man.

"Prime Minister," said Jerry in his clipped, modulated voice that reminded people of Ronald Colman. "I was on Lord Mountbatten's staff. You may not remember this, sir, but I received you on many occasions. Jeremy Jackson is the name" and then, most uncharacteristically for an Englishman, he clicked his heels in the manner of a Prussian colonel of the hussars, and bowed his head with a jerk.

"Ah, yes, Mr Jerkson" said Panditji absently. When the process was repeated with Mrs. Gandhi, who was accompanying her father, she looked straight through him. It was clear that neither of them recognised him from Adam.

Then one day Jeremy Jackson disappeared – without a word of warning, he just wasn't there anymore. I asked Sir Robert McPherson, his Ambassador, about this. "Just pushed off" he replied. "Sent us a note in the mails forfeiting his right to a month's salary in lieu of notice and asking that the price of a single return fare to New York should be paid to American Airlines when they sent the bill – this too against his account, of course."

Sir Robert knocked the ashes out of his pipe and went on: "Mysterious chap, really. Never got to know much about him. Was appointed by my predecessor on the strength of a letter from someone high up in the Foreign Office. Ah, well, awfully nice chap and all that, but God knows we had little enough use for his India-Pakistan expertise."

So I asked my old friend, Merrivale Peterson II, Minister-Councillor at the American Embassy, if he could look into Jeremy Jackson. We had been together in previous posts and were thick as thieves. They have swarms of CIA people and other agents in their foreign service, and I wondered if they could solve the mystery. "Sure thing" said Merrivale, and he called me a couple of days later.

Jeremy Jackson, he told me, was the son of a leading garment manufacturer on New York's First Avenue, whose "Jackson jumpers" are perhaps as well known as Levis and other denim-type trousers. Revolting from the idea of spending his lifetime in a tailoring establishment, young Jerry had run away from home and, after a series of adventures in England, found service as a stoker in a mine-sweeper, surviving several U-boat and dive-bombing attacks at sea. The end of the war found him in Calcutta, from where he had bummed his way to Delhi and worked for a year or two with a firm of men's outfitters known as Ranken's. Now his father had died and left him with twenty million dollars, and as there was no one to run the family business, he had acknowledged the call of duty. This, then, was what Merrivale told me; but how it reconciled with Jerry's exploits at school and varsity and in the Eighth Army right through to the Viceroy's House – I will never know.

I, myself, received orders of transfer some months later, and just about that time each of our daughters received for Christmas an embroidered Jackson jumper, and inside the parcel was a card on which Jerry had scrawled the following lines by Robert Herick :-

Gather ye rosebuds while ye may,
  Old time is still a-flying:
And this same flower that smiles to-day
  To-morrow will be dying.

*

The ultimate freedom

Whenever freedom of the press is mentioned – and when at the same time expressions like newsprint allocation, price-page policy and diffusion of ownership are bandied about – my mind goes back to the time, nearly thirty years ago, when this great concept was first formalised.

In pursuance of a resolution of the Economic and Social Council (ECOSOC), the United Nations Conference on Freedom of Information was inaugurated at the UN's European headquarters in Geneva in the spring of 1948. The session lasted four weeks and was attended by delegations representing fifty-four Governments, plus observers from three other Governments, and consultants from eight inter-governmental and non-governmental organisations. On the basis of its deliberations, the conference, apart from adopting 43 resolutions, prepared and forwarded to ECOSOC draft articles for the Draft Declaration on Human Rights and the Draft Covenant on Human Rights.

India sent a varied and colourful delegation, brilliantly led by Sir Ramaswami Mudaliar. To say that they made a good impression would be putting it mildly. They played an important and effective part in the deliberations of the conference, and their contribution inspired an American commentator to report that "leadership at international conferences is noticeably shifting from West to East and in this leadership India is playing an outstanding role."

Sir Ramaswami's role was, of course, predominant. A lonely-looking figure, he was yet conspicuous – his squat-sitting turban and the marks on his forehead being one of the reasons – and his counsel and advice were much sought after. In a brilliant inaugural speech during the discussion of the basic tasks of the press and other media of information, he made his call for a code of honour for journalists, which subsequently received world-wide interest and acclaim.

"My people and Government believe in freedom of information" said Sir Ramaswami. "They want to ensure complete freedom of information as far as possible, subject only to those well-understood limitations bearing on public morality, public decency, and the ordinary state of the people themselves – limitations which are intended to serve the purpose of ensuring the freedom of the individual for which a free press exists. Beyond that we do not want to lay any limitations... Is it too much to expect that the time has come when a code of honour may be drawn up for the learned profession of journalism?"

Sir Ramaswami again scored a personal triumph when, against strong United States opposition in the final plenary session, he secured inclusion in the projected United Nations Covenant on Human Rights, a provision allowing Governments to prevent by law "the systematic diffusion of deliberately false or distorted reports which undermine friendly relations between people and States."

Sir Ramaswani declared that it was far from the idea of the Government of India to use the provision in order to impose restrictions on the press. "The Indian proposal is inspired by a policy of good-neighbourliness" he said. "There may be people and countries where, for a certain time, in certain circumstances, it may be desirable to see that systematic and deliberate distortion of facts should be prevented."

There came the time when – part of hoary tradition – the delegations had to entertain each other. For our first function, for various reasons, Sir Ramaswami decided to invite the principal delegates of the Eastern European countries. "Arrange a hearty meal for them," he told me. "This thing I know I can leave in your good hands."

Geneva at that time was a gourmet's paradise. Although the war had ended three years earlier, many capitals, notably those of countries which had been ravaged by the conflict, still lived under austerity conditions. In London, for example, the fare provided was dull, monotonous and unappetizing – usually a solitary course of some kind of fish or a boiled meat, with boiled potatoes or boiled beans as the only accompaniment. But here in the Swiss capital everything – but everything – was freely available, including lashing of thick clotted cream and ladles of thick creamery butter; crisp long stalks of celery and tangy red radishes, strawberries, peaches, grapes, melons – names which to many of us had become merely a memory.

I took Sir Ramaswami literally and went about arranging our luncheon in my usual conscientious fashion. Even though I knew something about the eating habits of the Russians and Poles and Czechs, I made further diligent enquiries and ordered a menu which I was certain would make any comrade water at the mouth. It was a long time ago, but I remember that, apart from the various aperitifs and canapés, we started off with a borscht, that most satisfying soup from the opposite corner of Europe, this followed by an exquisitely broiled sturgeon, then roast suckling pig and saddle of lamb with béarnaise sauce, all these accompanied by appropriate wines and finally champagne – a meal, I thought, fit for the Czar of all the Russias. The Pole on my left nodded approvingly, and so did the Hungarian on my right, and as I looked round the table I noticed that our guests were literally drooling as they wiped the grease from the corners of their mouths.

After the guests had left, I went over to Sir Ramaswani, relaxing in an armchair, a glass of Perrier at his elbow. "It went off rather well" I suggested to him. "Our friends seem to have had a good tuck-in."

Sir Ramaswani slowly sipped his mineral water and gave me a look. "Yes" he admitted "it went off well, as you say – apart from one omission." He paused as if to catch his breath. "It seems you neglected to find out that I am a strict vegetarian. I myself hardly swallowed a morsel." Beneath his swarthy complexion I could see that he was livid. "We are here to discuss human freedoms. One of the fundamental freedoms is freedom to eat — only you stretched this a little and took upon yourself the freedom to decide what others should eat."

3

Embrace your gifts and encourage others to do so too.

I have lived my life according to many maxims, and I find the following by B.K.S. Iyengar the most useful in that one may substitute the first word for any of one's choosing. I often have and it has worked well.

"Yoga teaches us to cure what need not be endured
and endure what cannot be cured"

Thus spoke the Swami

Quite by accident, I came across an old friend in the book store the other day. Browsing through the paperbacks, I found a volume entitled "Autobiography of a Yogi" and was about to buy a copy when I remembered that the author had given me a copy in the original American edition; and when I got home, there it lay languishing on one of the shelves.

Swami Parmahansa Yogananda had presented it to me. He was one of the first, if not the first, of the itinerant Hindu ascetics to popularize yoga in the West. As early as 1925 he opened the Self-Realization Fellowship atop Mount Washington in Los Angeles on a site he said he had seen years before, in a dream.

Soon he had a following of many thousand Americans, among them movie stars and millionaire industrialists. Thanks to their munificence, he set up other centres, among them several Churches of All Religions, one of them housing a Mahatma Gandhi World Peace Memorial, and a headquarters ashram on a breathtakingly beautiful property overlooking the Pacific Ocean at Encinitas, twenty-five miles north of San Diego. The practice of yoga was, of course, basic in all these institutes, but incidental to them were a series of vegetarian restaurants where the public was introduced to a concoction known as the mushroomburger, or a meatless hamburger.

Leafing through the yellowing pages of that presentation volume, I was assailed by a flood of memories. I had accompanied the Ambassador, Binoy Ranjan Sen, on his first official tour of the West Coast in 1952. After the usual visits to the film studios and the University and meetings with prominent businessmen and members of our community, we went to the ashram on Mount Washington.

The Swami and a group of his inmates were waiting outside the entrance to receive us, all of them barefoot and clad in saffron-coloured robes. The smell of incense and the chanting of hymns floated through the air in our direction from some inner sanctum. Yogananda was graciousness itself, conducting us around every inch of the complex during a long morning. Twenty-four hours later he was dead.

As part of the programme, the Swami and the Self-Realization Foundation had invited the Ambassador to luncheon at one of the city's leading hotels on the day following our visit to the ashram. The banqueting hall was filled to overflowing, with people and flowers. At the head table I found myself wedged between a movie idol and His Grace the Bishop, I think. After everyone had eaten, Yogananda got up to make his speech. The theme was the brotherhood of man and the need for different peoples to understand each other better. He eulogized the country of his birth and that of his adoption, and the words "My India, My America" were on his lips when suddenly he clutched at his throat and fell back into his chair. Several doctors were in the audience and one of them, a disciple, tears in his eyes, announced that the Master was no more.

For three weeks Yogananda's body lay in state and it was noted that, despite the passage of time, it remained in a condition of perfect preservation, without any visible sign of physical disintegration. His followers, who gathered from far and near to pay their last respects, ascribed this to their departed leader's divine powers, but there were skeptics who asked that if the Swami could preserve himself in death, why was it that he could not have saved himself from untimely death itself? They also pointed to the fact that modern embalming processes had been developed to near-perfection, thus insinuating all manner of hanky-panky. Whatever the validity of their arguments, the Mortuary Director of the Forest Lawn Memorial declared in a notarized statement that it was "the most extraordinary case in our experience" and that "our astonishment increased as day followed day."

*

The Yogi and the blonde

Sometimes I wonder what happened to Birger Larsson. We had had some good times together and had promised to keep in touch wherever our respective careers might take us. He was an up-and-coming fellow who obviously was going to go places. Then his wife ran away with another man, and he just went to pieces.

Brigit Larsson was one of those blondes who might have walked right out of an advertisement for the Scandinavian Airlines. On the golf course her drive often exceeded mine; and I hit a pretty hefty ball myself. At the swimming club, when she jumped from the high board, you suddenly understood how the swallow-dive got its name. She was lithe and lissom and quite indefatigable. She could dance for hours on end and was always the last to want to go home.

How or why Birger and Birgit ever got hitched up will forever remain a mystery. They were as opposite to each other as the North Pole is to the South. He was tall, dark, gangly and bespectacled. A bookworm and an intellectual, he had topped every exam for which he sat, and it was predicted of him that he would end up either as Foreign Minister or die from overwork. From all accounts, the first hasn't happened to him, and I hope the second hasn't either - not yet, I mean, for death must come to all men. We were about the same age, and I was rather fond of old Birger.

I feel guilty, too, as in a way, I was responsible for the parting of their ways. We were sitting outside the club house at Tandjong Priok one sultry afternoon, all of us limp and dead-beat after four hours in the killing heat of the Javanese sun - all of us, that is, with the exception of Brigit, who was still fresh as the proverbial daisy. To burn up some of her remaining energy, or perhaps to quench it, she did four quick lengths in the pool and then plonked herself on one of the deck-chairs beside me. Then, tinkling the ice-cubes in her lemonade, she asked me: "Tell me, what is this thing you have in India called yoga?"

This was, of course, before the Maharishis made of it the thing it has since become - before Greta Garbo and Yehudi Menuhin lent their names to it, before The Beatles and Mia Farrow were lured into one of the Uttar Pradesh ashrams, and before New York and Los Angeles had sprouted yoga academies more numerous than in Calcutta and Bombay. Transcendental meditation did not yet belong to the language of the beautiful people, and Ravi Shankar was still to become more popular in the West than in his own country.

"Tell me about your yoga system," she repeated.

"Well," I replied, "we've had yoga with us since the beginning of time. Open any of our illustrated classics and you'll see sages and holy men in all manner of yogistic postures - asanas, I believe they're called. I remember my grandfather sitting cross-legged for hours on end, contemplating the plaster peeling off the wall and listening to the birds and the bees. Once in a while he'd stand on his head. For myself, I couldn't sit cross-legged for thirty seconds to save my life - and as for standing on my head, seems like I'm doing it all the time."

She pulled her chair closer to mine. "Now you're making fun of me," she protested. "But I'm dead serious. I want to know all there is to know about this thing you call yoga - about those exercises and meditations that make all ladies look like movie stars!" She went on and on until I remembered Pandit Thakurdasji who had walked into the Embassy the other day and told me that he was inspecting sites for likely centres for his Yoga and Divine Guidance Institutes, as he called them.

The long and short of it is that I arranged that Brigit should meet the Panditji at our home on the following afternoon. She arrived wearing one of those sheath-like garments that gave her a sort of penitent look. She had done her golden hair in plaits, and there was a long string of beads dangling from her neck.

The Panditji and Brigit were introduced.

"The thing you must remember," he told her, "is that yoga is an ancient science that brings harmony - physical, spiritual and sexual. To achieve this, the practitioner must have faith - faith in his science, faith in his teacher, and faith in himself. He must also remember that yoga is unlike any other form of exercise he has previously practised. In western callisthenics, the end result is that energy is depleted; in yoga, energy is restored. But the physical thing is only part of it - can you find peace and quiet in a gymnasium? Some of my pupils come to mock, or perhaps for a diversion; they stay because what they achieve is peace of mind. Now, there are a few basic postures that you must practise every day…"

After some demonstrations, they discussed the hours for her class and the fee for each lesson, and by the time these were settled night had fallen and the frangipani tree in our compound was giving off its sweet jasmine smell.

Two weeks later I was summoned to the Foreign Office by the Secretary-General. I had recently become Charge d'Affaires, and this high official had a stern look on his face. "It's about your visitor, the yoga expert," he said. Reports had come to him that a well-known lady's car was to be seen outside the Panditji's room in the Hotel des Indes until the early hours of every morning, and people had been talking. In view of the impending State visit of our Vice-President, he said, it became doubly desirable to avoid even the breath of any scandal. I was aware, he continued, of the high regard his country had for mine, for which reason no action had been taken against this visiting alien, who was being treated as a Government guest. Madame, of course, enjoyed diplomatic privilege; but I was her friend and her husband's, and as the other party was obliged to listen to my counsel, I should have no difficulty in handling the situation.

This sort of business bothers me, so that evening I went to talk it over with my next-door neighbour and long-time friend, Mohamed Roem. He was in the wilderness then (later he became Foreign Minister), we had got to know each other at The Hague some years earlier at the time of the Round Table Conference and again when he was sent there as Indonesia's first High Commissioner. Dr Roem brought out a bottle of my favourite whisky - although he didn't touch the stuff himself, being a strict Muslim, he was a generous host - and we mulled the matter until it was time for me to leave. "Sleep on it, my friend," he advised me. "You will require patience, and resolution, and tact, to tackle this delicate task, and for all these rest is of the utmost importance."

In the morning I sent for the Panditji. He was surprised and hurt. "I see the lady only in the morning," he said. "The fixed hours are from ten to twelve. She is a good pupil, and has paid all her dues in advance. About her nocturnal activities, I know nothing." Honesty was written all over his face and it was patent that there had been a mistake.

I then nipped over to see Birger. His nose was buried in a book, which he put aside when I entered. He poured me a stein of lager and we talked about this and that. I asked him why he had been in hiding for the past fortnight. "It's this report I'm writing," he said, "about the socio-economic future of South-East Asia. The Ministry want it before the end of the month and I've been burning the midnight oil, as you might say. Brigit has been looking after the social side and she tells me all that's worth knowing." If he was aware that anything was amiss, he didn't show it; and he was not a good actor.

Brigit called me the next day. Could I see her at once on a matter of some importance? We arranged to meet in the bar of the Hotel des Indes and at a corner table she began by saying that she would be eternally grateful to me for introducing her to yoga. It had cleared her mind and opened up new vistas. The Panditji had been wonderful and she would recommend him strongly to all her friends.

"Yoga has made me see that Birger and I are quite un-suited to each other," she went on. "We must go our different ways. And for the first time I have fallen in love - really in love." He was a travelling business-man from India who combined in his person all the attributes she had always looked for in a man. He too was a devout yogi, and they had been practising new postures every evening at this very hotel where he was staying. They were catching the plane for Bombay in the morning, and would then go on to a place in the south called Ooty. Birger has his books - and they have always been his greatest solace and most intimate of companions."

Birger Larsson, as I said, became a nervous wreck. He never finished his report on South-East Asia and even tore up the pages of his first draft in a fit of melancholia. Some time later he applied for a transfer to Helsinki. That was the last I heard of him.

*

The Godman of Golgonda

Bhagwandas and I were inseparable while at school and later, in our last year at college, we shared a room in the New Hostel. Neither of us was up to much in class, but at least he excelled in sport and might have captained the hockey eleven if he didn't have so many distractions. I basked in the sunshine of his popularity.

One night in our final term, as I was putting away my books and preparing to go to bed, he bought back with him two student nurses from the Medical College. Then he produced a bottle of rum and we proceeded (in his words) to have a ball. Word got out of our escapade and we both might have been rusticated, but he pulled some strings. Bhagwandas always had the right connections.

When we passed out – both of us by the skin of our teeth – we went our separate ways, and about the time I was preparing to go abroad, someone told me that Bhagwandas had floated a film company.

The years rolled by, and towards the end of my stay in the USA my work took me to Boston, where I stayed with Christopher and Mary Cromwell. I finished my business in a single day, but the Cromwells pressed me to stay over the week-end, and on Sunday morning Chris said to me: "We're taking you on a busman's holiday. There's one of your countrymen around. He's a sage or some such thing. Some call him The Guru, others The Master, but to most folks he's just plain Mr. Godman. He lives about sixty miles from the city limits, and it's a nice ride. Besides, the sun is shining."

"He comes from a place called Golgonda, which I believe is a township in your province of Andhra Pradesh," said Chris as we set forth. "People ascribe unusual powers to him. They come from all over the States merely to have his – what is the word? – darshan. He looks at them for but a minute, and they say that peace and solace descends upon them."

I've seen many impostors in my time – the world of holy men is full of them – and I have an unerring instinct for their shenanigans. Immediately I smelled a rat, but I couldn't let the side down, so I agreed to go along with my friends.

"I thought this type of person was concentrated on the West Coast" I said. "What made him choose the bleak climes of Massachusetts, where you can get snowed under for weeks on end?"

Christopher pondered the question. "California is already overcrowded with seers" he replied. "The climate there draws them – it's much like some of your own parts, I'm told. Over here he has no competition and, with due respect, he's cashing in on the fact. True, he does some good deeds – contributes to hospitals and schools – but let's face it. He's gotten rich in the process, is loaded, in fact. At present he's engaged in completing a temple that he has named the House of God. He has raised a million dollars for this from within his own following."

It was a beautiful ride - that I'll admit. There was a nip in the air but the sky was a clear blue, with only a few cotton-wool clouds floating lazily in its wide expanse. Slowly we negotiated our way through the bustling Bay area and then, leaving the shimmering azure waters behind, coasted on a freeway so smooth it might have been made of marble. No wonder they have so many traffic accidents in this country, I mused: their roads are made for speeding and every American seems to feel that he's entered for the Grand Prix!

All too soon the rolling countryside gave way to reveal a cluster of modest dwellings, amidst which were the usual drugstore, motel and cinema; and plumb in the centre of these a monstrous pagoda-style building, gold spires and all, standing out from the others like a sore thumb. The locals may have regarded it as typical of the exotic, mysterious East, but in fact it was an eyesore – I can think of no other word – whether or not it had cost a million dollars.

There was a hush as we entered the hall. People in their Sunday best squatted uncomfortably on a king-sized Persian carpet, making a mess of the creases on their trousers. There weren't many people that day – about forty in all – and we eased our way into places in the third row from the front. There was the smell of incense. Somewhere a cymbal clashed. A conch-shell called.

Then a curtain parted and the holy man entered, holding his right palm in a straight line from his nose as if about to execute a coup at karate. Ashes were smeared all over his forehead, over-painted with vermillion marks. He was clad in saffron-coloured robes, of course. Everyone folded hands and bowed low in their seats. I did likewise.

When I raised my head and looked at the figure now reclining against a bolster on the rostrum, I found myself looking at the visage of – could I be mistaken? – my old friend, Bhagwandas. He had developed a paunch and had lost or shaved off his hair; but I would have recognised him anywhere. No amount of make-up could disguise my companion of so many boyhood years. I looked away in confusion.

The Guru again raised his right hand and uttered a sonorous "Ohm!" Then he sank his chin upon his chest as in meditation. When he opened his eyes, he fixed his gaze on his audience, one by one, as if trying to identify each individual. Following each such inspection he uttered another "Ohm!", then passed on to the person next in line. When at last he settled on me, I thought I saw the flicker of a smile on his lips – and then he winked at me!

In about thirty minutes it was all over, and through a stereo system came the refrain of some film music of the "Hare Krishna" variety. This was the signal for all to leave, and slowly the congregation started filing out after a final respectful look and 'pranam'[6] in the direction of the figure on the dais.

"Amazing!" said one of them. "I'd never have believed it," said another. "An utter calm has descended on me – what a wonderful man!" said the lady on my right. Then as I myself passed through the main portal, a beautiful attendant in a white cotton sari with a "tilak" on her forehead, slipped me a piece of paper. It said: 'See me after your lunch. Come alone. It won't take long. – B.'

The Cromwells took me to the drugstore for lunch – a chicken sandwich and a glass of milk, which is as satisfying a meal as anyone can want – and when they suggested that they'd like to take a nap at the motel, I told them that I'd go and have a few words with the Godman from my country. "You do that" said Chris, "have him wash all your sins away!"

I strolled up to the temple, a bare five minutes' walk. The attendant was at the door and took me to an inner sanctum, where Bhagwandas awaited me. He hugged me warmly. "Hiya, fella", he said in a broad Brooklyn accent, "long time, no see." Then he told me his story.

---

[6] A bow (in respectful greeting).

The film venture had flopped, he said, and he was sitting around the studio at a complete loose end wondering what next to do, when a travel guide came along with a party of American tourists in tow. Among them was a script writer from Hollywood, a girl named Barbara. It was a case of love at first sight. To cut a long story short, they got married at a Registry Office and left for the USA a month later. Yes, that was the girl who had received me at the gate and, earlier, had given me his note. Wasn't she a peach?

"Barbara had already scripted a story about the holy men of India," Bhagwandas went on. "A sub-plot portrayed someone like me. That's how I came to be a Godman. Don't snicker – I'm not doing anybody any harm. On the contrary, many think I am doing a power of good. What can I say if people believe I can cure them of their ailments? Besides, I've made a good living, and Barbara and I are happy here."

*

The touch that heals

In the late summer of 1946 I found myself in London with time on my hands. The whole of the previous night I had been hurtling across the wide Atlantic in an RCAF Constellation via Goose Bay, Labrador, and those who complain about today's airline facilities should have travelled in one of those contraptions. They don't pamper you in a military transport plane.

Seven or eight months earlier I had been sent to Canada to open an Information Service in advance of the diplomatic mission which came into being the following year. Then, out of the blue, came this frantic instruction requiring me to stop everything and proceed post- haste to Paris, where I had been appointed PRO[7] to our delegation to the Peace Conference.

On arrival at Hendon I was informed that there wasn't an onward berth until some time the following day and that, for my convenience, a suite had been booked for me at the Grosvenor House. This

---

[7] Public Relations Officer.

Mayfair – Park Lane stuff may sound very posh and fancy, but I recall that when I was there, there was only a remnant of a cake of soap in the bathroom, that the solitary towel was grubby and in tatters, that the sheets had served several previous occupants, and that the breakfast, when at last it arrived, comprised a mess of powdered eggs and a rasher of bacon that tasted like shoe leather. There wasn't any hot water either. New Delhi, a long time and distance away, seemed like paradise; and Toronto like very heaven itself.

I was still unshaven, when the telephone rung with an insistent clamour. It was the hotel manager. "Excuse me, Sir," he said, "but something urgent has come up. I wonder if you would be so kind as to step into my office for a few minutes?"

Despite the austerity of those days, the manager sported a white carnation in his buttonhole, no matter that the cutaway coat and striped trousers were somewhat the worse for wear. He jumped from behind his enormous desk to greet me and directed me towards a distinguished-looking lady sitting all huddled up in one corner of the room. When we were introduced, she hastily dabbed at her eyes with an already sodden handkerchief and gave me a watery smile.

"It's about my daughter" said Lady Hetheringway without further ado. "Ever since she's been a tot of six she's suffered from these awful headaches. They come only once or twice a year and at any odd time, but they knock her out completely and the poor darling goes into a coma and is lost to the world for days on end. The doctors are mystified, and the Harley Street specialist who came this morning says that he's never known a case like this one."

She paused to stifle a sob, and I made a sympathetic grunt, wondering what on earth this had to do with me. Then she went on: "Every other night I have a dream, and in the dream a wise man from the East appears in front of my Lucy and he places the palm of the right hand on her brow, and immediately she awakens into good health. Again I had this dream last night, and when I mentioned it to Mr Lambert here, he told me about your arrival and I knew that this was an omen. Oh kind sir, please take a look at my little girl – please!" and she dabbed at her eyes again.

I pulled myself up to my full height. "Madam", I said in my most formal tone, "I happen to be an Indian civil servant, not a miracle man. True, I hold a doctor's degree, but that is in another discipline.

Besides, I believe your Medical Council has laws against charlatans and impostors."

She looked at me with red-rimmed eyes. "I beg of you" she implored me. "Perhaps you yourself are a parent. I assure you that no one will blame you, and if you can help my baby... please try to cure her – I have no one else to turn to" and she turned her face and struggled with her handkerchief.

I am by nature a soft-hearted man and a woman's tears can play havoc with my resistance. So I followed, meekly wondering what to do, with Mr. Lambert, the manager and obviously an old family friend, leading the way. On the third floor we got out of the lift-cage and walked towards a suite at the end of the corridor. There Lady Hetheringway took hold of my elbow and led me into a bedroom. The curtains were drawn, but a table lamp spread a glow all round, and on the pillow I noticed a shock of flaxen curls and under the eiderdown the gentle heaving of someone breathing. Then the door closed behind me.

Gingerly, I sat down on the edge of the bed, feeling as foolish as a lama in a girls' dormitory. How, I pondered, had I allowed myself to be led into such a situation? And then I recalled my parent's wish that I should become a doctor, prompted by my grandmother's belief that I had unusual hands with definite healing powers. To satisfy their whim, I took biology as a subject for my degree examination, but had then drifted away from it all, until I found myself where I was today – in the proud capital, albeit rundown, of history's most powerful empire, my whole life ahead of me and the world at my feet. What was I complaining about?

Gently and with new-found confidence, I placed my right hand on the girl's brow. Slowly I stroked her forehead, then placed my other hand behind her neck and pressed firmly in both directions. I lost count of the time when I heard a sigh – or was it my imagination? – And then some moments later I felt a tremor. Then she stirred. "Mother!" she called, and then louder: "Mother!"

Later in the morning the desk clerk called to inform me that a seat had been made available on the evening flight for Paris, and would I please be ready to leave the hotel at three? As I was checking out, I noticed Lady Hetheringway seated in the lounge, accompanied by her daughter. They came up to me. "Lucy wants to thank you personally" said the older woman. "She has never felt as well as she does today."

4

Observe people and learn

An evening with Howard Hughes

Las Vegas must be seen to be believed. It glistens at the edge of the Nevada desert like a rose in the wilderness, a living translation of the word 'oasis'. Here man has transformed a stark wasteland into a veritable temple of pleasure. Often have I wondered what might not be done to open up other barren regions, at home and abroad, given similar imagination, ingenuity - and money.

It was late in the evening when we arrived there after the long road journey from Los Angeles via the Grand Canyon. Some California oil magnate had suggested that we see a bit of Colorado and the rugged neighbouring countryside before returning to Washington. When the Ambassador agreed, he promptly provided an air-conditioned Cadillac sedan and a uniformed chauffeur who knew the territory like the palm of his hand.

Along the way, the driver, a former USAF pilot who asked us to call him "Butch", told us something of Nevada's boom-and-bust history. Exposed to the vicissitudes of Mother Nature it had known many ups and downs, and in the early part of the century, in an effort to restore its sagging fortunes, its elders legalized gambling. The effect was electric - people started pouring into the State from all parts of the USA; and when they went further and passed into law the residency regulation for divorce, the whole place began to burst at its seams. The divorce law was no great hardship, Butch remarked: after six delightful weeks, often spent on a luxurious dude ranch, freedom from wedlock was automatic.

Paradoxically, said Butch, it was easier to get married in Nevada than in any other American state. If the girl was at least 18 and the man 21, and if they could both speak or signal the words "I do," all they needed was a licence and a justice of the peace to become man and wife - no residency requirements, no blood tests, no delay in performing the ceremony once the licence was obtained, the latter being as easy to get as a coke from a drug-store. Thus was it, said Butch, that Nevada became the great marriage-and-divorce factory of the USA.

He had just finished telling us this, when suddenly the desert ended and we approached what looked like a fairyland. Along the avenue known as The Strip, dancing neon signs in red, green and blue lights transformed themselves into shapes and words proclaiming the varied attractions of Las Vegas, mainly gambling and dinner revues, available at the city's many luxury hotels - The Flamingo, The Desert Inn, Caesar's Palace, Sands, The Lotus Inn, The Golden Nugget and others too numerous to mention, each the acme of tourist comfort and elegance.

We ourselves had been booked at the resort's newest hotel, named The Thunderbird, and there a representative of the Governor was waiting in the lobby to receive us and take us to our rooms and to inform us that he would call at eight in the morning to escort us to the temporary Executive Mansion. Then, he said, he would take us to see the Hoover Dam, one of the world's great irrigation and power projects, 700 feet high and impounding one of the largest man-made lakes anywhere - Lake Mead, which is 110 miles long.

The Ambassador pleaded a headache and retired to his suite, saying that he would call room service for dinner. That left me on my own, which suited me fine. It was a long time since I had been exposed to what is commonly described as a fleshpot, and I wanted to make the most of the opportunity. But things did not turn out quite the way I might have wished.

Another thing about Las Vegas is that the various casinos make so much money from the gambling that the hotels can afford to spend fortunes on diverse indulgences whereby to lure more and more visitors. Thus, because of the profits, the prices are kept low and gargantuan full-course dinners, with star-studded floor shows thrown in, can be had for less than half the price obtaining in, say, New York or Chicago. At that time Jimmy "Schnozzle" Durante, Ethel Merman and Frank Sinatra were appearing in different rooms of this one hotel alone - each one of them a front-ranking name commanding thousands of dollars for a single performance.

For a while I wandered around the huge lounges on the ground floor, the rooms furnished in impeccably good taste, with long-legged, scantily-clad waitresses passing around trays of drinks and canapés - all on the house. Tentatively I tried one of the slot machines, or "one-armed bandits" as they are called, and as luck would have it, at the third or fourth try three lemons stared me in the face - jackpot! And with a crash a quantity of small change fell into the till below. I crammed the coins into my two pockets and took them to the counter, where another luscious lady gave me silver dollars in exchange.

I was nursing a mint julep and trying to make up my mind where to eat - the Sinatra room or the Merman room? - When a dapper, tuxedoed stranger came up to my table and greeted me politely by my name. He sat down by my side and introduced himself as Alistair something or other, "secretary to Mr Hughes." When my eyebrows shot up in inquiry, he added: "Mr Howard Hughes - perhaps you have heard of him, Sir?" It was like asking if I had heard of Dwight D. Eisenhower. Howard Hughes was perhaps the most fabulous American living - millionaire, magnate, inventor, aviator, producer of hit films, discoverer of glamorous stars, chairman of blue-chip companies, and eccentric recluse. It was rumoured that he owned half of Las Vegas, where at present he was in residence, occupying the entire top floor of one of his luxury hotels. I would have given my right arm just to shake his hand.

"Mr Hughes" the stranger explained, "has heard of your arrival. These days he is very much taken up with the study of Oriental religions and philosophy. He would like very much to meet your Dr Radhakrishnan, and is prepared to make a special trip to India if such an interview can be arranged. With this in mind, he requests that the most excellent gentleman with whom you arrived give him but thirty minutes of his time. The difficulty is that Mr Hughes keeps somewhat unusual hours - he can make himself available only between midnight and one o'clock. Could you help me to oblige my master, sir?"

I told him that the most excellent gentleman had retired for the night and that it would be more than my job was worth if I were to disturb him at this time. He pondered this impediment, and then asked: "I wonder if you would be so kind as to accompany me, sir?

All he wants is advice, and Mr Hughes might find it instructive to have a chat with you. You could perhaps give him some of the information he wants and recommend some reading material, etcetera."

Now, I have never regarded myself as an expert on Hindu philosophy, nor any of the scriptures for that matter, but I have been trained to bluff myself out of such situations. This I could do by animatedly relating episodes from the 'Mahabharata', so much so that people can be quite impressed, or so they say.

There, I shot my plans for the night, but what the heck? A meeting with the mysterious Howard Hughes was worth all the fleshpots of Sodom. I nodded my assent and, as it was already past eleven-thirty, accompanied the stranger to a waiting limousine. Minutes later we were outside another neon-lit, multi-storeyed edifice. A private elevator sped us to the penthouse floor, on the landing of which heavily armed guards passed us into a waiting room of unbelievable elegance.

Blow-ups of film stars covered the walls - I recognized Jean Harlow, Jane Russell and Paul Muni: Howard Hughes had made them famous. Soft music played in the background, and a butler brought in a tray of drinks. The minutes passed; then the wall in front of us crackled and, as if on a cinema screen, a picture began to appear. It developed into the visage of the great man himself. He wore a striped pyjama jacket, and a gauze mask covered his mouth - Mr Hughes was noted for the precautions he took against germs. Then his voice spoke. "Alistair!" it shrieked, "I said I wanted to speak with the older gentleman, not this one!" Then the picture faded and the room was silent.

Wordlessly, my companion took me back to my hotel, his face a study in dejection. Despite the bright lights and the prevailing gaiety, I was no longer in the mood for making whoopee. Besides, I had to get up early.

That was how I never got to meet Howard Hughes. I was sorry to read of his death the other day. Now I will not get another chance to meet him.

*

The making of a president

"Whoever holds high office," Richard M. Nixon once said to me, helping himself to another pickled onion, "must have a sword of Damocles dangling over his head every moment of the day and night. The work-load kills him as surely as death by assassination. No, siree – that's not the life for me. This is as far as I wanna go. What I look forward to now is a future filled with serenity."

That was in 1951. We were seated around a buffet table at the Indian Embassy in Washington, and he and I had been discussing the recent British general election in which Clement Attlee had been defeated and Winston Churchill returned to power. We had talked about the fickleness of public favour and the ups and downs of political life. He was a Senator then, having recently moved up from the House of Representatives, and I had asked him if he aspired to the highest office his country had to offer. "No, siree" he repeated. "This is good enough for me. I wanna have a good night's sleep, every night of the week. Nobody with great responsibility ever gets more than a wink once in a while. What is it that Shakespeare said - uneasy lies the head that wears a crown?"

I remember telling him: "That's not quite correct, Senator. We had a man in our country who carried the burdens of millions of our people over a long period, and I don't recall anybody mentioning that sleep was any problem with him. Rest he didn't have much of, but when he closed his eyes, I'm told he slept like a babe."

"Ah, but Gandhi," replied Nixon - "Gandhi never wore a crown. A cap of thorns maybe, but not the crown of public office. That makes all the difference. Do I want to hold the highest post in these United States? Oh, brother! They can keep it for themselves, so far as I'm concerned."

Some months later Nixon was named by Dwight D. Eisenhower as his running mate and in due time, despite an early setback, he became Vice-President of the USA, which post he held for eight years. Not quite the highest office, true, but more was still to come. Before leaving the Eisenhower administration, he took a crack at the Presidency, being narrowly beaten by John F. Kennedy, and when he ran for Governor of California two years later he was roundly defeated by a political lightweight, Pat Brown. That was when he declared publicly, something he'd told me privately ten years earlier but in different words: "If anyone thinks I'll run for office again, he's off his rocker." He was kidding, of course, because it was crystal clear to all with eyes to see that his whole life and purpose was dedicated to occupying the Oval Office in the White House in Washington, DC.

On one occasion, shortly after our first meeting, I mentioned to him, apropos of something he had said, that our Prime Minister had made a broadcast on world government entitled "A Crisis of Spirit" and - man of crises that he was himself - he asked if I could let him see the text. When I got to the office in the morning, I got my secretary to make out a copy and send it to Mr Nixon in the Senate. I met him again perhaps a month or two later, and we found ourselves in the corner of a large diplomatic reception. I asked him if he had read the paper I had sent him, at which he looked me sternly in the eye and recited: "We live in an age of crisis. One crisis follows another and, even when there is peace, it is a troubled peace with war and preparation for war. Tortured humanity hungers for real peace..." He went on for five minutes, reproducing precisely, word for word, the opening paragraph of Mr Nehru's broadcast in that baritone voice that was to become familiar to millions over radio and television - a. little masterpiece, a prodigious feat of memorization, which won my immediate admiration.

"Bit of a dreamer, your Nehru" Nixon said, pronouncing, the name 'nee-rue'. "Lives mostly in the air. But some of his ideas are right - the world hungering for peace, for example. I go along with him there. And if I ever get a chance, that's the area where I'll concentrate - the search for peace in the world, in our time, for our children and for our children's children."

I asked him if he had ever met our Prime Minister. "Briefly" he replied, mentioning some function he had attended during Panditji's first visit to the USA in 1949. "I'll tell you something" he added, drawing closer as if about to take me into his confidence. "I didn't take much of a shine to the fellow. Kow-towing to China and Russia - one day he'll get his comeuppance. And what the heck is this thing he calls non-alignment? Well, every country gets the leader it deserves - good luck to you with your Mr Nee-rue."

My dislike of Richard Milhaus Nixon dated from that moment; and I was in good company because even then his enemies were calling him 'Tricky Dicky' and in that early stage of his career he had more enemies than friends. Already he had earned the odium of liberal Americans because of the manner in which he had hounded Alger Hiss and Whittaker Chambers in the anti-Communist hearings conducted by the House Committee on un-American Activities, and at that time he competed with Senator McCarthy in the unpopularity lists.

He never concealed his aversion towards India, and this manifested itself openly at the time of the birth of Bangladesh. I never could understand his bias in favour of Pakistan, until I was told that he felt he had been cold-shouldered during his first visit to our country while, on the other hand, in Karachi he was treated like the Caliph of Baghdad! Petty he was, and mean, and throughout his life and career and even as President - specially as President, because Watergate was the offspring of meanness and pettiness - he showed time and again how low he could stoop to gain an advantage or take it out on an enemy, real or imagined. Yet when I listened to his resignation broadcast on that fateful morning of 9th August 1974, I felt sorry for the man.

And so it came to pass that Richard M. Nixon's head was toppled by that very sword of Damocles which he professed so much to fear.

*

The maximum leader

One of my most prized mementoes is a polished cigar box with the Cuban coat-of-arms depicted in full colours on the lid and an inscription stating that it was presented by Fidel Castro to his "amigo" - myself.

It came into my possession in this manner.

After presenting my credentials to President Dorticos, I told the Foreign Minister, Raul Roa, that I was anxious to meet the Maximum Leader before I left Havana to return to my headquarters in Mexico City. For good measure, I requested an appointment with Che Guevara also. Dr. Roa studied his fingernails with some deliberation, and then replied, "I shall try."

When I mentioned this to my colleagues who were resident in the Cuban capital, they pooh-poohed the very idea. Castro, they said, had not granted an interview to a foreign diplomat, other than the Russians or the Chinese, for over a year. And as for Guevara, well, he had become as rare a specimen as a burra sahib walking down Chowringhee in a sola topee.

I forgot about the matter, and for the next few days concentrated on enjoying myself. For in the Cuba of those days, despite the American blockade and other nuisances, there was much to enjoy for those with eyes to see and, more important, with minds to perceive. True, such goods and services as make life worthwhile in westernised society were in desperately short supply or non-existent, but there was still the bright blue sky and the broad golden beaches fringed with waters which changed from emerald green to deep purple as the sun progressed. That much, at least, Batista had not been able to take away; nor the smiling faces and graceful, easy-going ways of the people.

Youth was the dominating feature of Castroland at that time; youth, and straggly beards and olive-green uniforms and hobnailed boots. Gone were the Fifth Avenue fashions of yesteryear and, in smart stores once bursting with merchandise of every description, the shelves were bare. If anyone complained, it was the dispossessed, those older people whose magnificent villas now served as schools or hospitals or hostels for the young. The Bay of Pigs was a past episode, a subject of derision, and the missile crisis was still some months ahead, tucked away in an unknown future. Today a certain electricity seemed to touch every member of this new generation. 'Libertad' was the password, and the swanky but deteriorating Hilton Hotel where I stayed was now known as the Havana Libre, and the popular drink was called Cuba Libre, a mixture of excellent rum and ersatz Coca-Cola.

They gave me a colossal Cadillac to run me around, but this proved something of a white elephant as it was constantly conking out. "No spare parts, señor" apologised my escort, a protocol officer still in his teens. The driver shrugged his shoulders and patched up the errant carburettor somehow, and in fits and starts we arrived at a seaside resort some fifty odd miles away from the capital.

A former luxury hotel, once the playground of American millionaires and their mistresses, was our destination. There, in a cabaña facing the shimmering ocean, we watched plump, bronzed children frolicking in the sand. A bus unloaded a group of land girls and, when they changed into bikinis from their ugly dungarees, it was pleasing to note that the revolution had not been responsible for any deterioration in the female form divine.

The sky was rosy pink and blue, and a subdued breeze rustled through the spiked fronds of the palm trees. There was balm in the air, and the scene was so exquisitely beautiful that my ill temper, brought on by the tantrums of our wayward chariot, disappeared like magic.

"Que bonito!" I remarked to my companion, practising my phrase-book Spanish.

"Si, señor. Gracias" he replied laconically.

We went into the elegant dining-room, and the maitre d' arrived with a menu approximately the size of a newspaper. Unfortunately, most of the courses had been scored out; but there was still the plato-del-dia, and on this we had no choice but to settle - a spicy if watery concoction made up of shrimps and seaweed and a lonely potato which had settled at the bottom of the tureen. It wasn't exactly a gourmet meal but, as my grandmother once taught me, I made appropriate noises and gestures to make them feel that I had eaten a meal fit for a king.

Some hours and several breakdowns later, back in my hotel room in Havana, I was resting my weary bones and my poor stomach, when the telephone rang and a feminine voice informed me: "Commandante Guevara, he receive you in fifteen minutes. I wait for you in lobby. Yes?"

At the appointed time I was shaking hands with about the most good-looking, bearded man I have ever seen. He was wearing crumpled drab fatigues, but the way he carried his uniform, it might have been the latest creation from a bespoke master tailor.

Che Guevara had then divested himself of the Finance portfolio to become Minister of Industry, but he combined a variety of diverse functions. It was around this time that he started preoccupying himself with a complicated experiment to diversify Cuba's one-crop economy - a venture which was to prove a disaster and perhaps precipitate his departure for the jungles of Bolivia where he was due to meet his untimely death.

What we discussed is probably still available in the archives - I hope it resulted in due course in some increase of trade, if nothing else - but as I took my leave I asked him about his impressions of India, which he had recently visited. He took a long pull at the inevitable cigar, looked heavenwards in deep thought, and rattled off something which was quite incomprehensible to me. The interpreter put this into polite language, but in plain words it was simply this: "You have about the most goddamn awful meat in the world." This need not be taken as an insult because Guevara was, as may not be generally known, a native of Argentina, a country as proud of its livestock as the British are of the Rolls-Royce engine. He could, I was told, eat an ox for breakfast (if he could get it) and what he must have been served in our various guest-houses is a matter which makes one shudder.

Next morning I started thinking about my departure. Although I had only twenty-four hours left, I had not quite given up hope of meeting the Prime Minister. Our reputation was still pretty high in those days, and our representatives abroad were shown a consideration which sometimes bordered on discrimination.

Sure enough, as I was messing about with one of my suitcases, a young warrior with a wisp of beard and a pistol dangling from the holster at his waist, knocked on my door. Commandante Castro, he told me, had returned from a tour of Oriente Province, and would receive me now. I was then taken by a devious route, criss-crossing through by-lanes and back alleys, to a rendezvous I could not again identify for a million dollars.

The Maximum Leader was standing in the doorway, a foot-long cigar clenched in his firm white teeth. "Mucho gusto, señor embajador" he said as he crushed my hand and led me towards a sala. When he discovered that my Spanish was only elementary, he said, "No importa, I speak like you." After he had dismissed his aides, he discussed in passable, if hesitant, English almost every subject under the sun. He exuded vitality and self-confidence, but for some absurd reason reminded me of Henry VIII.

For the next two hours, to the accompaniment of interminable cups of syrupy black coffee, he rambled on. He talked of shoes and ships and sealing wax, of cabbages and kings - and U.S. Presidents. He puffed away as he spoke, pausing only to replenish the tiny cups. When he asked me, "you no smoke?" after I had declined for a second time the preferred cigar, I explained that in our country we abstained, as a mark of respect, in exalted or venerable company. "Ah, so!" he said, nodding his head in comprehension.

As I was about to board the Aeronavis de Mexico plane the next morning - incidentally, the only service permitted at that time between Cuba and the American mainland - a youngster in battle-dress and wispy beard brought me a package tied up in red, white and blue ribbons. It contained the box aforementioned, and in it were row upon row of the fattest, longest Havanas you ever saw. On each subsequent visit, two or three times a year, a packet of refills was delivered to me in my hotel room or at the airport, with the Maximum Leader's compliments.

Now only the empty box remains - and my memories.

*

A man named Menon

One of the most glamorous of our Independence Day celebrations was held at India House in London on the 15th of August 1948 – glamorous, not in the sense of fashionable clothes and expensive jewellery, because England then was still licking the wounds of war, but for the galaxy of notables and talent present. Atlee was there, and Pethick-Lawrence; Stafford Cripps and Bevin; the crème de la crème of the ruling Labour party, among them but still unknown, an individual someone introduced to me as Harold Wilson. Barons of industry, service chiefs in full regalia, editors, authors, actors – everybody who was anybody was there.

I spotted a group of pretty young ladies gathered some yards away from the receiving line, intently studying High Commissioner Krishna Menon and Lord Mountbatten, concentrating on them as if they had been commissioned to do a memory sketch at the end of the party. "What's cookin', good lookin'?" I said to one of the girls in the vernacular of the era. She frowned at me, then apparently relented, and told me that she and her friends were comparing notes to decide who was the more handsome of the two – Menon or Mountbatten!

Even his worst enemies conceded that Krishna Menon had brains the size of a watermelon – but a matinee idol! That flummoxed me completely. The High Commissioner, I'm afraid, was never very fond of me, as I had been appointed to his staff against his preference for someone else, but this incident gave me a new conception of the man and after his comparison with Mountbatten, however ludicrous, I could never reciprocate the ill-feeling he seemed to harbour towards me.

V.K. Krishna Menon was one of those people you either loved or loathed. There was no middle way about it. But whatever his critics thought about his methods – and these were regarded as devious by some and downright objectionable by others – no one denied his dedication to duty, nor his loyalty and patriotism.

My first encounter with him took place in circumstances which were not exactly propitious. He had become our High Commissioner in London and I had been appointed to his staff as head of the Public Relations Department at India House. I remember that I broke out into a cold sweat when I received my transfer orders in Canada, where I was then serving and doing very nicely, thank you very much. In Delhi in those days a wisecrack was going round the South Block that the Government in India was suffering from "Meningitis" and that, of all the Menons who had moved into the higher echelons, Krishna was the one to be avoided like the plague. Although this was a promotion for me, I tried to wriggle out of the appointment, but then wiser councils prevailed; and now here I was in the great man's outer office on a bleak winter's morning, waiting to be summoned into the presence.

He looked up from his papers as I entered the room and motioned me to a chair. He pushed aside the tea tray that was in front of him, scowled at me and barked: "Well?" I introduced myself, referring to a letter I had sent him from Ottawa, pledging my utmost devotion in the work he was directing. "What letter?" he snapped. "Nobody shows me anything around here." But when I saw his private secretary after the meeting, he produced the letter with the initials "VKK" scrawled on it. "Don't worry" said the secretary, "this happens all the time."

Some days later Gandhiji was assassinated and all bedlam broke loose at India House. During the tumult, I received a visit from one of the directors of Madame Tussaud's, the famous waxworks museum. They wanted to put up an effigy of the Mahatma, he said, and for this purpose they required several blown-up photographs from different angles and also specimens of articles with which the dead man was identified – loin cloth, wooden sandals, spectacles, timepiece, charkha[8], etc. As the pouch was leaving for Delhi in the next few hours, I put in an urgent requisition to the I & B Ministry.[9]

Three or four days after this, I was summoned to his upstairs office. A cipher message had arrived calling for further details regarding some of the items I had asked for. "Why was I not informed?" the High Commissioner enquired. "This is a matter of topmost priority, and only I should have handled it. A message from me to Sardar Patel would have been more effective."

About this time I had been passed a copy of a telegram informing the High Commissioner that I had been appointed Secretary-General of the Indian Delegation to the Freedom of Information Conference opening in Geneva in a few weeks time. Apart from myself, the services of Sir Dhiren Mitra, the Legal Adviser, and some members of the clerical staff had also been requisitioned. We had few missions in Europe in those days and, as these were sparsely staffed, the Government of India depended increasingly on the facilities available in London.

Krishna Menon was furious. "How the hell do they expect me to run this place!?" he said, or words to this effect, as he flung the pink cipher despatch across the table. "At least they might have the good manners to consult me in advance when they propose to denude me in this manner." This was a slight exaggeration, as India House was then staffed by about 1,500 people and the shifting of a handful here or there hardly made any difference.

I seemed always to be at loggerheads with the High Commissioner, and it was clear that my days with him were numbered. He had dumped a variety of old India League hands into the PR Department, most of them totally unsuited to the tasks they had to tackle. With calculated patience and tact I got him to move them elsewhere, and in one of his most gracious moments he said to me: "Whatever else, I must admit that you are a good negotiator." Nonetheless, when I was serving with our delegation to the United Nations General Assembly

---

[8] The portable spinning wheel invented by Gandhi.

[9] Ministry of Information and Broadcasting.

in Paris, I got a letter from him to the effect that he was heart-broken, but the Ministry had seen fit to transfer me to headquarters and as he did not want to stand in the way of my advancement he had reluctantly agreed to the change, failing to mention that as my replacement he had succeeded in getting someone he had wanted in the first place. He even gave a small farewell party in my honour, and when I went to take my leave of him, he spoke to me with an uncharacteristic show of affection.

I worked for a year and a bit in the United Nations Division of the Ministry of External Affairs, at which time I met Krishna Menon fairly often. He had become Defence Minister but, whatever the designation, he was de-facto Minister of UN Affairs and Joint Foreign Minister. No important decision was taken without his approval, and in his favour it must be stated that he was always firm and forthright in his opinions. That was the period when delegates of powerful nations trembled when he took the rostrum at the United Nations, where he had become a hero to all of Africa because countries of the continent were becoming independent one after the other, and it was at the UN that he pleaded their case with this special brand of oratory.

He was a kind man, fond of children. He was not a good picker of people, but those he picked he backed to the hilt. And when his downfall came after the Chinese debacle of 1962,[10] he took his dismissal like a man, without recrimination, without rancour. At no time did he utter a word against Jawaharlal Nehru, whom he worshipped, and in the bitter days when he was in the wilderness, he remained tight-lipped where smaller fry would have lashed out in all directions to vindicate themselves.

Krishna Menon made mistakes, but he had vision. How much of our military preparedness is due to him, few people will ever know, but it was he who laid the foundations of the infrastructure on which the indigenization of our defence production is based. A mutual friend, an American journalist, once described him to me. "Krishna," he said, "is like a lion in sheep's clothing." I had no reason to be fond of him, but I wept on the day when I heard that he was no longer in our midst.

---

[10] The Sino-Indian War, 1962.

The peripatetic Punjabi

Sucha Singh hobbled down the ramp somewhat unsteadily. It wasn't his age, I was sure of that, as my octogenarian friend was as tough as they come. But it is usually a bumpy flight from Tijuana to Mexico City – a distance greater than that between Calcutta and Bombay – and planes were slower in those days than they are now.

He had sent me a telegram the previous day, saying that he couldn't let me leave the country without him saying a personal "adios." And now here he was, walking up to me. In one hand he carried a small valise and in the other an airlines bag containing, I discovered later, his special copy of selections from the Guru Granth Sahib, wrapped in blue silk cloth.

His visit wasn't exactly convenient, as we were all packed up and ready to go; even though my British colleague, Sir Peter Garan, offered to put him up, I couldn't think of such a thing. So, hurriedly, we readied one of the guest rooms, and I believe Sucha Singh was comfortable for those two days that he stayed with us. He wasn't a fussy person.

Both days were crowded with farewell functions, and Sucha Singh came to all of them, matching drink for drink and revealing an appetite that might put a youngster to shame. And the energy of this frail-looking man! "How do you do it?" I asked him out of sheer exasperation, and he replied: "Simple. The secret is not to fret – take things as they come." This is good advice for an impatient world seemingly in a hurry to get things done before the bomb explodes.

There was one place where he drew the line, however. He would not eat beef. The Mexicans pride themselves on their steaks and to decline this delicacy is like saying "No" to Johnny Walker when he offers you a peg of his Black Label. I asked him about his abstention in a man as liberal as himself. "I promised my mother" he replied simply, "and that's one vow I've never broken."

"But you drink like a fish – surely your mother didn't recommend alcohol in large doses?" Sucha Singh smiled, but gave no reply.

After his busy first day with us, after I was preparing to go to bed, he said to me: "What's the hurry? It's so seldom I get to speak to a Punjabi." So I pulled out a bottle and we settled down in a corner of the drawing-room behind a pile of trunks and other paraphernalia.

"What goes on in the old country?" he asked me.

I pondered the question. So much had happened that I didn't know where to begin. The Chinese had humiliated us on our north-eastern border, for example, and Prime Minister Nehru was reported to be seriously ill, some believed mortally.

"Much is happening" I replied. "Both good and bad. In the last twelve-month period we've been administered a shock or two, but old Bharat Mata will survive. She always has."

My answer did not satisfy him. "But who will take over when Panditji goes? Is there anyone else? How about his daughter? Surely people like yourself must be worried?"

I hate discussing politics at the best of times, and forecasting has never been my forte. I shook my head. "Who knows? They asked the same question when Roosevelt died. And Stalin. But America and Russia carry on. And so does England without Churchill and France without de Gaulle."

"What about the young lady?" he persisted.

Again I shook my head, and then made a pronouncement that has haunted me ever since, showing me up as a poor judge of people and events.

"Mrs. Gandhi isn't interested in politics" I told him. "I've had a chance to watch her at close quarters recently and the impression I get is that she's too shy a person for the rough and tumble – even afraid, you might say. Certainly she has no ambitions so far as government is concerned. In any future calculation, I would not put her in the picture at all."

He asked about food production and social reforms and job opportunities and the pace of education and… but when he saw me stifle another yawn, he took the hint and knocked back the contents of his glass. "Buenas noches", he said and I escorted him to his room.

Among our engagements the next day was a "charriada" – a sort of miniature bull-fight – which the local authorities had arranged in honour of my wife and myself. It was mostly a display of horsemanship and no bulls were killed, although the participants went through all the motions. Our two teenage daughters were bubbling with excitement, as two of their friends, both amateur "charros", were taking part and performing special antics for their amusement. Sucha Singh sat through it all with a long face. "This aspect of their culture has never appealed to me" he told us later. "Cruelty I could never stomach, whether to man or beast."

Immediately after this there was a "comida" at Relaciones Exteriores (the Foreign Office) to which Commonwealth Ambassadors and senior Government officials had been invited, and at which the Foreign Minister presented me with a heavy silver tray engraved with the signatures of all heads of departments with whom I had been in contact over the past four years. This was in lieu of the decoration – the Golden Order of the Aztec Eagle – to which all retiring Ambassadors are entitled but which our regulations prevented me from accepting.

Sucha Singh was seated between the Chief of the United Nations Division and the Ghanaian Ambassador, and I was pleased to notice the aplomb with which he conversed with both. When the Minister, Señor Manuel Tello, got up to make his speech, he gracefully included a reference to my friend and to the contribution that early immigrants from India had made to the Mexican economy.

There were other receptions later in the day, including one by the diplomatic corps, and finally a dinner given by my own Embassy officers and staff. At the latter function, Sucha Singh joined in the chorus of post-prandial orations by making a speech in which he mixed several languages with equal abandon. "Bhayo aur beheno", he began and then, breaking into English and making a play on the translation of my name, referred to a "gem of purest ray serene", and ended up by referring to those assembled as "Señoras y Señores" and wishing them all "Hasta luego".

I was dead beat when we got home and Sucha Singh noticed this. He also knew that we had to be up early to be at the station at seven. The new rule requiring all officers on transfer to proceed by plane had just been introduced, but I had obtained special permission to travel by the surface route, first by train and then by steamer. Alas, those good old days are gone forever! Never was there a more relaxing holiday than a lazy cruise between, say, Bombay and Tilbury Docks or Southampton and New York. Days, and sometimes weeks, were spent in pampered comfort, with gourmet meals and diverse entertainment included in the price of the ticket, and an entire army of stewards and others existing only for your greatest convenience. What, apart from speed, do today's jet monsters have to offer by comparison?

When the time came to say goodbye, Such Singh embraced me warmly in full view of the large crowd assembled at the station – an action quite without embarrassment because the "abrazo" is the common salutation throughout Latin America. His eyes were moist and there was a lump in his throat when he said to me: "You take my good wishes, of course. The nightingale sings for you and you will have music wherever you go. You are one of those lucky people who spread happiness around. Go with God, my friend."

*

The painter's lady

Rummaging through an old suitcase the other day, my wife came across a Mexican pocket diary which unmistakably had once been mine. Its pages were mostly blank, as I've never been much good at maintaining these little red books, but there were two conspicuous entries, written in my handwriting on different days of the month. They said simply, and identically: "Meet Emma."

Now here were the classical ingredients of an incipient domestic imbroglio. The words were discriminating enough, hinting at secret assignations with a mysterious paramour, may be in Chapultepec Park on a moonlit night or elsewhere under the shadows of Mount Popocatepetl. But there was nothing so sinister here. My wife merely smiled and said: "Wonder what's happened to dear old Emma?"

Emma Hurtado de Diego Rivera was one of our earliest friends in the Mexican capital. The second living relative of the famous muralist painter, she had already been a widow for several years when she first invited us to her home in the Calle Ramon Alcazar in the old quarter of the city. The house was a veritable museum and many of the old master's paintings, each one a priceless work of art, adorned its walls, while others lay carefully stacked in a spare bedroom. Although Diego

Rivera is now mainly remembered for the monumental frescoes he executed in the Palacio Nacional and other public buildings, he was a versatile and prolific craftsman, applying paint and brush to anything that came his way, and most of his smaller work is to be found only in private collections in different parts of the world.

I remember now the reasons for those entries in my diary. Mrs. Gandhi was due to arrive on an official visit – this was, of course some years before she entered the government – and somehow I had got the authorities to agree that one of the functions should be a luncheon hosted by Señora de Diego Rivera. Emma, I should explain, was something of a lone bird: an individualist, and not in particularly good odour with the establishment, which regarded her as a communist – most establishments dub those who don't agree with them, or don't pander to them, as communists or revisionists or worse. The guest list had to be carefully checked, therefore, and other details gone through with a fine tooth-comb, but the resultant "comida" was delightful for its informality and intimacy and was one of the highlights of Mrs. Gandhi's tour.

Emma was no longer a beautiful woman, if ever she had been beautiful. She had been a striking redhead once but now, after a frequency of "treatments", her hair always reminded me of a string of carrots. She was putting on weight in the wrong places. But there was no kinder person than Emma Hurtado, and no more gracious hostess.

We became, as I said, good friends, and many were the evenings when her diesel-driven Mercedes could be seen outside our house on the Avenida de Las Palmas or our Buick Roadmaster outside her door in the old city. And on several occasions we stayed with her in Acapulco in the villa her husband had left her, overlooking the great bay. She had renovated and modernised this, and I believe we were the first occupants of the guest wing she put up alongside the new swimming-pool. While the tourists and others beat it up in the fleshpots of this fashionable resort city, we would sit out there till the early hours, chewing the rag until the cerveza and the tequila ran out.

On one such evening our conversation turned to beautiful women and their hold on famous men through the centuries – those femmes fatales who had become historical figures in their own right. My wife pointed out that beauty had nothing to do with it. Cleopatra, she said, had a hooked nose and Lady Hamilton was so fat she tipped the scales at thirteen stone. Catherine the Great, who had more lovers than any known seductress, measured fifty inches around the hips and Nell Gwyn had short, bandy legs.

I don't know where she got this information, but she went on like a faucet that can't be turned off. She switched to the present day and informed us that Elizabeth Taylor had "rolls and rolls of adipose" and that princess Grace of Monaco, the former Grace Kelly of Hollywood, "was practically blind, my dear" and could not recognise the man seated across the table from her without the aid of thick-lensed spectacles. No, she said, it wasn't beauty alone: it was something that had been described by various generations as "it", "oomph", "sex-appeal" or just plain "personality."

Possibly I had drunk one too many tequilas, but suddenly I looked her in the face and asked: "Tell us Emma, what did you have which so attracted Diego? What was it that made America's most famous painter seek you out from all the women from Montreal to Montevideo?"

That was a silly question because, of all things, Diego Rivera was no chocolate-box artist. His murals spoke of revolution; they depicted tyranny and oppression and death; they mirrored the struggle of the common man against the social order. If anything, his subjects were miserable creatures – both in his frescoes and in the smaller canvases, the layman's general impression is one of ugliness and squalor. I believe our own Satish Gujral came strongly under his influence during one period.

Because she did not answer, I pressed on: "Was Diego very much in love with you, Emma?"

Emma asked me for a cigarette, and blew out a cloud of smoke.

"What did Diego see in me?" she said softly, "I have often asked myself the same question. God knows I was no ravishing beauty. He became used to me I guess." She paused while she stubbed her cigarette into an ashtray. "What was it the English poet said?" she asked. "Beauty lies in the eye of the beholder. In those words perhaps lies the answer." She looked into the distance as if in a trance. Then she cleared her throat and recited in her guttural voice:

Ask not of me, love, what is love?

Ask what is good of God above;

Ask of the great sun what is light;

Ask what is darkness of the night;

Ask sin of what may be forgiven;

Ask what is happiness of heaven;

Ask what is folly of the crowd;

Ask what is fashion of the shroud;

Ask what is sweetness of thy kiss;

Ask of thyself what beauty is.

Some days later Emma took us to the Dolores Cemetery in the capital. Here in the Rotunda of Mexico's Illustrious Sons lie the mortal remains of Diego Rivera, and precisely on this site his widow has lovingly built a monument to his memory. The centre niche is a mosaic depicting an Aztec girl in prayer, candles and other offerings surrounding her solemn, squatting form. As we stood before this simple yet spectacular mausoleum, Emma turned towards us. Her eyes glistened with tears. "This is the story of my love," she told us.

*

What's in a name?

Some said he was born with a silver spoon in his mouth; others that he had the golden touch, whatever that might mean. The fact remained that he prospered in every situation. He was envied by some, disliked by most, respected by all. Because of his westernised ways and the manner in which he got on with his superiors, mostly with foreigners, he was described as a toady and dubbed "The Brown Sahib." His name was HG Wells.

For those who may be dubious, I suggest they look up the Army List of 1933 and there on page 211 they will find the entry: "Wallis, Har Gopal. b. 1908; ed. Government College, Lahore, and Royal Military College, Sandhurst…" Apparently he was one of those chaps, and there were quite a few in those days, who believed there was an advantage in giving an Anglo-Saxon twist to his name, and no harm done if it resembled that of a famous novelist. A subsequent issue of the Gazetteer confirmed that his new appellation had been "legalised by public notification."

It was as HG Wells, therefore, that Har Gopal Wallis was taken into the Political Service from the Army and, with the advent of independence, seconded to the Foreign Service. Already by that time he had acquired a record of some distinction, having scored equal success with the Afridis in the Frontier Province as with his masters in the Imperial capital. As a reward he had been sent on brief junkets to China and South Africa, from both of which he returned with additional feathers in his topee, if that is the expression.

No wonder, they said of HG Wells, that he could charm the hind legs off a donkey. Give him a warring tribesman, and he made him a lifelong friend. He was at home in any place as in the ruggedness of the Gobi Desert. But where he excelled was with his note on file. Once, the Secretary of his Department asked him to comment on the growing agitation in favour of Prohibition. "All things considered, it must be conceded that the situation is very fluid" he wrote in his immaculate script below a rambling discourse recorded by an underling, his Section Officer.

As happened to other talented people at the time, HG Wells was made to accept something of a demotion when he joined the Ministry of External Affairs. He was started off as an Attaché and Personal Secretary to the Minister of State, but he so distinguished himself with the organization of the first Afro-Asian Conference and the drafting of replies to condolence messages which poured in from all corners of the globe at the time of a national bereavement, that he was soon appointed a Deputy Secretary and later, over the heads of a dozen others, the Chief of Protocol. In the latter capacity the ambitious young diplomat was brought into touch with world leaders who jostled each other in arriving to pay their personal testimony to the fledging new democracy. These contacts were to stand him good stead.

From these beginnings HG Wells came to be a legend in his lifetime. Within a year he was transferred to the USA as Minister-Counsellor and in quick succession was offered almost every diplomatic post worth the name. Wherever something happened, Korea or the Congo, Indo-China or Egypt, there he would be; and readers with avid memories will recall pictures of him in the news magazines, standing discreetly behind or alongside Harry Truman and Mrs.

Pandit in Washington, Jawaharlal Nehru and Chou En-lai in Bandung, Gamal Abdel Nasser and Krishna Menon in Cairo, and one with General Thimmayya on a flight to Pyongyang. When he reached the mandatory retiring age, he was given an extension, but when he was proposed as Governor of one of the larger states he politely (and wisely) declined, recognising that enough is enough. He now leads a quiet life, tending his apples and cross-breeding them with his pears in the small orchard he acquired in the Kulu Valley just before he stepped down.

At the height of his meteoric career, I met HG Wells in one of those delightful packet-boats of the Java-Bengal Line which, in a more leisurely age, used to ply the placid waters of the southern seas. Those were the good old days when the "approved route", no matter what the distance or the time involved, was always by ocean liner. Nowadays our officers are required to fly post-haste, and I think many will agree that, with this transferral to the jet-engined aeroplane, much of the glamour and some of the attraction has been removed from the popular conception of life in the foreign service.

I was being transferred from Djakarta, and had just scrambled aboard after a hectic morning of farewells and those other necessary exertions that beset the departing traveller. HG Wells was sitting at the bar, cool as a cucumber, refreshed after the cruise from Hong Kong via Manila and Bali after a "trouble-shooting" mission to one of our eastern outposts. He could yet look forward to the second half of the journey; after a brief pause in Singapore for transhipment to the British India Line, Penang, Rangoon and Calcutta were still to come before he returned to the rigours of his desk in New Delhi. "A civilised way to re-charge one's batteries," was his comment.

I climbed on to the stool next to his and ordered a lager. He was sipping a Campari and soda, which had just become the fashionable midday aperitif, and when I noticed this, it made me feel like a country bumpkin beside a cosmopolite. But he quickly put me at my ease. "No better drink in the world" he said, pointing to my tankard, "and nothing like beer to quench one's thirst after the kind of morning you must have had." After my third Heineken - and he matched me with his Camparis - we were at peace with all men and went to lunch arm in arm, so to speak.

The band was playing *Oh! What a Beautiful Morning* as the majordomo led us to a portside table in the crowded air-conditioned dining-room.

No land was in sight any more, and shoals of flying-fish were pirouetting in the coral blue waters outside. A shapely young thing appeared before the mike. Although this was before the mini skirt, her knee-length dress left little to the imagination. She tossed her golden tresses and warbled the words of the Broadway hit song.

An excellent mulligatawny soup was followed by a Caesar salad and lobster thermidor - the Dutch feed you well on their ships - these accompanied by a most admirable Rhine wine, and by this time HG Wells was ready to survey the scene of his far-flung operations. I complimented him on a large and difficult loan he had negotiated some months earlier.

He put down his fork. "Foreign aid - baloney!" he said. "Crutches, blinkers, that's what it really amounts to. When will we learn to walk on our own feet and see with our own eyes?" He then launched into a tirade against the country to which he would soon be returning to complete the aforesaid transaction.

"Champions of democracy!" he said, taking a gulp from the glass at his elbow. "Has nobody yet noticed that they are champions only of the decadent, discredited dictatorships?" He took another gulp of wine. "Greed, self-interest and a total lack of morality - those are their watchwords" he continued angrily. "The only satisfaction is that they can't last much longer. Their system is finished, doomed. I give it fifteen years more, twenty at most. First the almighty dollar will begin to totter, then other bastions will come crashing down. Mark my words! You and I should still be around to greet the day…"

The talk had become a little too gloomy for my liking. The food and drink, and the prospect of two coming weeks in the lap of idle luxury, had given me a feeling of euphoria. The girl was now singing *Some Enchanted Evening*, and I wondered what she would be doing after dinner.

"Tell me, HG" I said, wanting to change the subject, "what is the secret of your success?" Much as a reporter might ask a local celebrity. He proceeded to tackle the mountain of strawberries which the steward had placed before him, dismantling at first the snow-line of ice-cream. He feigned to ignore my question. "They call you the man with the magic touch" I persisted. "Are all the tales about you true?"

At last he smiled. He crushed the last of the succulent red fruit between his strong white teeth, wiped his mouth and told the steward we would take our coffee in the lounge. There he produced a king-sized Havana, cut the tip carefully, struck a match, sat back in an armchair and stretched his legs.

"Magic touch, eh?" he said, blowing a cloud of smoke. "I've heard worse things said about me!" He paused to strike another match. "I've been lucky, I guess" he continued, "but magic touch, no. It's been a sweat. I've listened, and I've scribbled, and I've done a fair share of running around. Above all, I've learned to follow orders and think the way my masters are thinking."

His cigar had gone out, so he struck another match. "But I'll tell you one thing," he went on. "If there's been any magic about me, it's all had to do with my name, and I'm glad I hit on the right one when I did. Imagine if I had chosen, as someone once suggested, Henry Wallace! No, sir, HG Wells it was and HG Wells, by the grace of God, it remained. It has opened doors for me like a password. Nobody could resist seeing what I looked like – a great writer or a one-eyed chimpanzee - but, once seen, I was never forgotten. Don't ever believe the fellow who asks you, what's in a name? There can be magic in a name. There was in mine."

*

Painting the clouds

Adversity is something that afflicts all people at some time or another, and it is those who meet it with a smile who come out best in the end. In the struggle for survival, it is the tough guy who gets ahead fastest, and if the fellow's an optimist as well, he will last the course much longer.

As a boy I remember getting irritated by a maxim my father had the habit of repeating. He had picked it up someplace – from a book or at the theatre – and whenever someone had to go to the dentist to have a tooth pulled, or did badly in a crucial examination, or lost in the final of the tennis tournament, he would invariably say: "It's a great life if you don't weaken."

These words have followed me around the globe; and in due course I came to understand their wisdom. How many times might I have gone under had I not retained faith in myself, or had my sense of humour not come to my rescue, or had I not learnt the importance of acceptance? After all, it doesn't take much sagacity to realize that, of the billions of people who inhabit this earth, not all of them can reach the top or become playboys and millionaires.

Writing these lines made me think of Archibald Sheean. Although he didn't put it the same way, he was a man with my father's brand of philosophy. He was constantly humming tunes like "Blue Skies" and "Oh, What a Beautiful Morning!" And the clichés he used! At first I hated the sight of him, thinking he was a show-off and a fraud, but when I got to know him better, I changed my mind. In fact, Archie and I became good friends and he and his wife Jill still write to us at Christmas and sometimes in between.

I first met him at one of these diplomatic parties – you know, the usual jazz: buffet for a hundred people and booze, booze, booze! There I was, standing in a corner, plate in hand and struggling with a chicken breast, when this rumple-suited chap came up to me, some kind of regimental tie around his neck and a smirk on his face.

"Hi!" he said, offering me a little finger to shake between the crumpled chop and highball glass he was holding. "I'm Sheean. Archibald Sheean. My friends call me Archie. You must be the bloke just come from Delhi. Was out there myself at the fag end of the war. Couldn't stand the beastly place. Just not my cuppa."

Immediately I took offence, but his remark was directed, not against our nation's capital, but at the pen-pushing he was made to do after being invalided out of the RAF. I thought he was an awful twerp, and said so to the Embassy girl who was giving the party. She replied: "Who, Archie? He's all right. They just don't make them like him any more."

Archie was a sort of hero, I learnt later – one of Mr Churchill's original "few". When his Spitfire was shot down into the Channel after a sortie, they gave him a bar to his DFC[11] and when they fished him out of the brine, they didn't give him much of a chance. But

---

[11] Distinguished Flying Cross.

Squadron Leader Sheean had different ideas; and when he came back to old Blighty after R&R in the Orient, he was almost as good as new.

Meanwhile, Archie had suffered a series of personal tragedies. Both his parents had been buried under the debris when their cottage was hit in the early part of the blitz. An older brother, a corvette commander, was torpedoed in the Atlantic. His sister divorced her lieutenant-colonel husband because he turned out to be an alcoholic and a homosexual. At 24, he was alone in the world, with only a boxful of medals and paltry severance benefits to his name.

I never knew a fellow so prone to accidents. Shortly after our first meeting, his brakes failed and he crashed into a lamp-post on Dupont Circle. When we visited him in hospital, his face was swathed in bandages and they told us he'd broken a collar bone and several ribs and lost most of his teeth. When he smiled, there was a hole in his mouth. "Only a scratch", he said meekly.

Burglars broke into their house in Chevy Chase and decamped with almost everything they possessed, including a thousand dollars Archie had taken out of the bank in the morning. But he was worried only about his medals, and when he found out that these hadn't been touched, he broke out into such guffaws of laughter, one might have thought he had just won the Derby Sweepstake.

When we were transferred to Indonesia, he could see that this was not the posting of our choice. After all, it's a long hop from Washington DC to Djakarta, and the American way of life does tend to spoil one a little. He came to the ship to see us off. "Not to worry, sweetie", he told my wife. "It's a great life if you don't weaken."

All I want to add is that when he retired some years ago as an Air Marshall, Archie bought himself a farm in Kent. In the first season, a blight destroyed all the fruit on the trees. In the next, some disease wiped out most of the livestock and poultry. He and Jill have been in and out of hospital several times; but whenever he writes, he gives the impression that he's the happiest man in the British Isles.

5

Embrace your community and celebrate your identity.

"Man becomes great exactly in the degree in which he works for the welfare of his fellow men" Mahatma Gandhi

On several occasions I have pondered the subject of persons of multiple nationality - not merely those who can possess different passports, but also those who hold the same place in their hearts for both the lands of their birth and of their adoption. Many prominent people have elected to settle abroad, some even in our own country, but it is a remarkable fact that, Indian expatriates more so perhaps than any other community, preserve the closest attachment and affinity with their motherland.

All over the wide world you find them - in the Americas from Canada to Argentina (except Mexico, where the immigration barriers are too formidable) throughout Europe and Africa, and in diverse regions washed by the Pacific and Indian Oceans and the Arabian Sea, Doctors, lawyers, architects, students, teachers, tailors, holy men, seers - you find them everywhere. Their behaviour patterns may vary from place to place, and it is found that the humbler folk cling more firmly to the old mores and customs, but a common feature is their deep and abiding religiousness and patriotism.

Rich or poor - and some are very, very rich, while others can be very, very poor - in their homes the morning puja is regular ritual, and they observe the festivals as if they might still be in Baranagar or Baroda, not thousands of miles away. They eat the old familiar foods, of course; and even in New York's fashionable Park Avenue you are guided to your host's apartment by the culinary odours that permeate the building. And when old Mother India is in difficulty - be it a famine or a flood or conflict with a neighbouring country - they rally in aid of the common cause.

Breathes there an Indian whose pulse does not quicken at the memory of the 15th of August so many years ago? In one of history's great climactic crescendos, an entire sub-continent shook itself free of the bondage of centuries and, to the blowing of conches and the rolling of drums, moved from alien rule to freedom. It was the end of an era - a tryst with destiny as Jawaharlal Nehru put it in his own elegant way.

When Independence came there were many Indians who were not on their mother soil to celebrate the event. Hundreds of thousands of them - ten million, according to some estimates - students, settlers, traders, political exiles, holy men, travellers - were in foreign lands; but all of them participated in the national rejoicing in one way or another. India had formal representation only in a handful of countries- a High Commission in London and an Agency-General in Washington, for example. In many others, however, a variety of official or non-official missions existed, and all these celebrated the occasion appropriately, even though the charkha may have taken the place of the chakra in the middle panel of the tricolour and some people may have chanted *Bande Mataram* instead of *Jana Gana Mana*. It was thus an international observance in every sense.

In a faraway corner of the globe, in the Forest Hill Village district of Toronto, our ensign was unfurled for the first time in Canada over the residence of our senior official in that country, the India Government Trade Commissioner (to give him his precise title), Mr. MR Ahuja. I describe Canada as far removed because this was before the advent of the jet age and - as an aftermath of the war - shipping was still badly curtailed. It took me the best part of five weeks to reach the Northern Dominion, travelling by troopship from Calcutta to Los Angeles and thence by railroad via Chicago.

Mulkh Raj Ahuja stood not very much more than five feet in his woollen socks, but what he lacked in inches he made up in determination, drive and in an intense patriotism. India has today no better friend than Canada in the Commonwealth, and if our countries see eye to eye on so many of the world's problems, some of the credit must belong to pioneers like Ahuja who did so much to interpret our way of life and thought to alien peoples and describe to them our hopes and fears and dreams. He was something of a martinet: his staff trembled at his approach, but his office ran like a clock.

He was a terrific salesman, and in characteristic fashion he had invited everybody who was anybody to his function, and although there were difficulties of protocol and of distance - the Canadian capital is in Ottawa - a goodly crowd of three hundred or so, representative of all walks of life, attended.

For her part, Mrs. Ahuja had outdone herself and produced an array of savouries and sweetmeats which could read like a catalogue of North Indian culinary specialities. A variety of kababs were passed around, and papads and pakoras and samosas, and trays of pink and green and creamy confections made from carrots and almonds and pistachios, all these covered with silver leaf. But the hit of the evening turned out to be some bread she had prepared in the tandoor they had built in their backyard; this was intended for the evening meal, but one of the children had cut it up into little squares and - stroke of genius - offered these alongside small bowls containing maple syrup. The Canadians dunked the pieces of bread into the molasses, and the verdict was unanimous - delicious!

A gong summoned the guests to the garden for the main ceremony and, in a neat little speech, Ahuja recounted the things India and Canada had in common and others they could achieve by joint endeavour. He then referred to the maple tree, the leaf of which now adorns Canada's national flag, and the treacle derived from the concentrated sap of which has long formed part of the staple Canadian diet. He pointed to one of the long tables where empty dishes lay scattered alongside empty jars, and remarked: "See how your maple syrup goes with our tandoori roti!" Thus a new phrase was coined for the promotion of international amity – "Tandoori Roti Indienne avec Maple Syrup Canadienne."

In the Sudan, ten years later, the President of the Republic graced our home for a small private reception we gave to celebrate our independence anniversary (the official function is held on Republic Day). "Kull-lee, Sayed Safir" he said, "tell me, Mr Ambassador, how are things progressing in your great country?" Five months earlier I had accompanied him on his State visit to India, and he had been much impressed by all he saw. Such conducted tours, however, do not always present the whole picture, only the better side of it.

"Your Excellency," I told him, "I would be less than honest if I were to say that all the flowers are blooming in our Indian garden. As you have seen, in Asia we have built an infrastructure second to none.

Our scientists and technicians are regarded as among the best in the world. Our food production has doubled, and we are making vast strides in our war against illiteracy and poverty. Yet there is a long way to go. Some people say that we are too large a country, have too many people pulling in different directions; that the severity of our climate makes us lazy and too inebriated for hard work; that we lack discipline and a sense of responsibility. If these shortcomings were to be overcome, then we could transform our country into a veritable paradise. But how do we overcome these shortcomings?"

The President shifted his enormous girth to get closer to me, and the sofa on which we sat groaned under his weight. "I know your country and I have seen your people," he replied. I have the greatest admiration for their ability and their capacity. Fortunately you are blessed with outstanding leaders. Inshallah! the time will come when Allah, in His divine wisdom, will grant you the guidance you need to surmount the difficulties you have mentioned."

These words come back to me on this, another anniversary of our independence, and I ask myself: How much have we accomplished and how many of the dreams and ideals of our founding fathers remain to be fulfilled? If the Germans can do it, and the Japanese and the Chinese, if they can accomplish miracles of recovery by discipline, dedication and hard work, why cannot we do the same? Faith, it has been said, can move mountains - faith and discipline and sustained joint endeavour.

*

Showing the flag

The meeting was called to order, and the Ambassador's wife arranged the palloo of her sari and cleared her throat.

"Sisters," she said, "I have asked you here this morning to discuss arrangements for our Independence Day reception. I need not tell you this," she added, "but it is as much your party as it is the Ambassador's. All of us must, therefore, exert our utmost effort to make it a complete success."

Then she allotted to the ladies of the community in this faraway capital their various duties, grouping them into four culinary committees for the purpose. One of these, under Mrs Jain, was given the responsibility of preparing snacks (vegetarian); the second (Mrs Ohri) snacks (non-vegetarian); another (Mrs Ahluwalia) to make purchases from the market; and the fourth (Mrs Sanyal) to make "service arrangements", that is to say, borrow as many servants as possible to supplement the waiters who would be hired to look after five hundred people.

Thus Madame Ambassador got out of doing any of the dirty work herself, reducing costs into the bargain, and who could blame her, considering the pittance her husband was given as *frais de representation* – "Do you know, my dear, what our Swiss colleague receives, and the Brazilian, not to mention the American and the British… in fact all of them, except our poor cousins the Pakistani and the Burmese?"

Four and a half miles away, in his air-conditioned office in the heart of the city, His Excellency was presiding over a similar conference, attended by all India-based members of his staff, diplomatic and non-diplomatic, and the principal office-bearers of the local Hindustani Association. More committees were formed, one for lighting arrangements, another for the musical programme, yet another to supervise the car park, and a fourth to select ushers and the like. Most important of all, the confidential committee was asked to organise a nook in the Ambassador's study where whisky, sherry, chilled beer and suchlike would be available for those who found the non-alcoholic beverages prescribed by the regulations distasteful to their palates. The First Secretary, placed in charge, was given strict instructions enjoining him to be very discreet, and was warned that an entry would be made in his service record if anything went wrong.

Three weeks later, on the evening of August 15, the Embassy garden was transformed into a fairyland. Myriads of multi-coloured electric bulbs, carefully concealed, glittered from every bush and treetop. From some background came the plaintive wail of the strumming of the veena, interspersed with the occasional thumping of the tabla. White-jacketed waiters, laden with trays, flitted among the guests. The ladies wore their finest silks and chiffons and the gentlemen a variety of attire from formal evening dress and military uniforms (with medals) to business suits and black achkans with white churridars.

It was a sight to please the eye, except perhaps of the host, who tired easily on his feet – and was thirsty. He looked at his wristwatch. "Not long now," he said to his wife, smiling beside him at the head of the receiving line, as the first of their guests approached to take their leave.

These were the British Ambassador and his wife. Lady Pugnose put her arms around the hostess in a display of warmth most untypical of Britannia. "My dear, what exquisite eats," she said. "Those crispies, what do you call them? Pakodas? And those little triangular patties? Samosas? Mmmm – simply delicious. Congratulations, dear, you must have a wonderful cook. What's that – you made everything yourself? You Indians are so clever! Poor little me, Dick says I couldn't boil a kettle of water to save my life!"

Meanwhile Dick, her husband, was shaking the host's hand. "Jolly good show, old chap," he said. "Wish we could do ours like this, but they've cut us down to the bone. What's that you said – you used all your own money for all this? I say, that's jolly sporting of you, old man. And what a smart idea not serving any of the hard stuff. Gives the old liver a bit of a rest, what? Well, toodle-oo, we've got to run."

While escorting them to their Rolls Royce, Mr. O.P. Nanda, the Embassy Registrar and chairman of the sub-committee in charge of departing guests, overheard Sir Richard Pugnose say to his lady: "Now for a *real* bloody drink."

*

Long ago and far away

All the world over, in the Americas and in Asia and even in the wilds of Africa, you'll find Englishmen who still change into a black tie for dinner, start toasting the Royal Family with the soup, and send Christmas hampers to their aunt Bessies in Abbey Wood, Henley on Thames or Wolverhampton.

Whenever there's a world war – and we've had two such conflagrations in our century – they'll pack up their old kit bags, hike to the nearest British Consul and volunteer to be shipped overseas to fight for King and country

Such a one was Thomas Atkinson, who was head of the British Information Service in Washington when I arrived there as his opposite number in our own outfit. He had the usual clipped accent and a walrus moustache that concealed a stiff upper lip, and was already a major personality by virtue of the fact that he had appeared on the cover of Time after a poll conducted by that estimable magazine to determine the man most typifying the expatriate Briton. Earlier, after relinquishing the editorship of a New Orleans newspaper to join the BEF,[12] he had come out of Dunkirk with a game leg and a DSO[13] and was sent back to continue the good work he was doing with his American cousins.

At that time when it wasn't fashionable for us to say nice things about the British, he overheard me tell a group of mutual friends at the National Press Club that India was a better place because of the game of cricket that John Bull had brought out with him. Although Sunil Gavaskar had not yet arrived on the scene, nor Bishen Singh Bedi, I reeled off the names of C.K.Nayudu, Vijay Merchant, Lala Amarnath, et al, describing them as heroes of the Indian populace, adding those of Ranjitsinhji and Duleepsinhji and Pat Pataudi as rivals of W.G.Grace and Hobbs and Sutcliffe for popularity on their own home ground.

After this I could do nothing wrong so far as Tommy Atkinson was concerned and he threw open to me the extensive facilities of the BIS, which was no small favour because, although on paper we are supposed to have equal status, in practice the wherewithal provided by our benign authorities was like peanuts compared to theirs. Thus I was able to get more mileage out of my own tin buggy than had any of my predecessors, and the people back at headquarters thought I was quite a fellow.

As I said, Tommy and I became good friends and we were often seen at each other's place. He was genuinely fond of India, having had an uncle in Skinner's Horse who had served in Poon-ah, who had stayed behind after retiring from the Army and was now growing tea in some place called the Nilgiris. "Tell me about your caste system",

---

[12] British Expeditionary Force.

[13] Distinguished Service Order.

he would say to me out of the blue, or: "Is it true that your people pray to cows and monkeys?"

Meanwhile, Tommy would go about his business and I would go about mine, he lecturing about the mother of democracies and the rule of law and I about non-violence and the importance of means before ends. One day after dinner, as I was cupping a balloon glass of Napoleon brandy in my two hands, I asked him: "Tell me, Tommy, you think so much of the old country – what the heck made you want to leave home?"

He gave me a sad smile and replied: "Never could stand the beastly place. What with the rain that goes on and on and the fog and the smog and Atlee's bleeding socialism and taxes going up with every budget and all good Scotch reserved for export only and coloured immigrants crowding the best places – sorry, old chap, nothing personal, of course – Tommy my boy, I said to myself, east and west and home's best, that's all very well, but put an ocean between yourself and these beloved shores and see how much better old Albion looks from the other side. Well, you asked me – that's the sum of it."

*

No place like home

For Krishna Kumar, nothing less than a filet mignon was the very minimum. He had majored from a mid-western university and, wanting to linger on for whatever his reasons, was now employed by our consulate in New York as a local recruit. He was sent to receive us when we arrived on the Queen Mary; he took us to our hotel in his own Buick Roadmaster, and in the evening invited us to dinner at an inexpensive but good restaurant. We remarked about his car and his Brooks Brothers suit, and he told us that such things were easy on the "never-never" plan – all that was required was a moderate down payment, the balance in easy instalments, and start to worry when the time came to re-equip. We took an instant shine to him, and he must have impressed others in the embassy besides, because some months later he was transferred to Washington, where he was given the designation of Transportation Officer. This entailed a variety of chores, but where he excelled was in receiving and entertaining visitors, functioning as a junior sort of chief of protocol. He continued to live well but, as his popularity grew, he fell foul of the babus[14] from Delhi, who managed to get him fired under one pretext or another.

Undeterred, Krishna Kumar washed dishes in a cafeteria – it is possible to live comfortably in the USA doing such odd jobs – before he found himself a berth in the publications section at UN headquarters. He tired of this soon enough, and then joined a garage across the river in New Jersey, where he did so well that he was awarded the "Best Salesman" pin two years running. This is where he still was when we ourselves were moved, four years after our first arrival. Needless to say we had become good friends, and at the time of our departure he came on board to see us off.

Krishna Kumar kept in touch with us as we moved on from capital to capital, and I was not surprised to learn in due course that he had shifted his activities to Hollywood, to which mecca many ambitious persons migrate sooner or later. His first job was on the Paramount lot, where they were shooting a film of a best-selling novel involving maharajas, holy men and an itinerant American heiress. He was some sort of technical adviser, his main function being to instruct the cast on how to tie turbans or wear loin cloths, subjects in which he had no knowledge whatsoever. No matter; he proved a roaring success and the studios kept outbidding each other for his services, such as they were. This was the period of the alliterative star name – Marilyn Monroe, Brigitte Bardot, et al – and although his own was a natural, he changed the spelling to Crissen Coomar, which he said sounded sexier and had more "class".

I had by this time been transferred to Mexico and, having to perform an official duty in Tijuana in the far north-western province adjoining California, I obtained permission to leave my territory for two days and cabled Criss about my intention. He met me at the Los Angeles airport in a Cadillac as long as a city block, chewing on a Havana cigar proportionately about the same size.

Needless to say those dizzy two days passed like minutes; and when I left Criss I had no idea of the surprise he was about to spring on us.

---

[14] Government Officials.

Barely a month later, he got married – confirmed bachelors usually do. Thereafter every other year, however great the detour, Criss and Joan would stay with us in our various posts before flying on to Bombay for his regular visit to his ageing parents. We were specially touched when they came to Khartoum, which is no holiday resort by any stretch of the imagination.

Criss is now Vice-President of a company that makes and distributes films for television. He continues to visit India regularly, and always makes the long hop to look us up. When he was here last year, our city was in the sadly sorry state it seems to have permanently acquired. Because of the power cuts, he had to climb three flights of stairs to get to his hotel room. He twisted an ankle on the rutted sidewalk. The stench from the uncollected garbage rose to high heaven. It was not the best of times to ask why he had never returned for good and although I wanted to put this to him, I thought it was best to leave well enough alone. After all, I mused as I poured him a drink, he spends more over here each trip than he would earn in a year, and he was a walking advertisement for the land of his birth. I filled my own glass. "Cheers!" was all I said to him. "Many happy landings!"

*

Population explosion

Because of its vast potential, Africa is perhaps the most important land mass in today's developing world; yet it is a sad truth that, despite the lip service we have paid to it - Jawaharlal Nehru was the foremost of Africa's champions - few of our administrators have wanted to serve there. In the Foreign Service, for example, so far as I can recall, only two ICS[15] officers - and it should be remembered that, until recently, the ICS was regarded as the crème-de-la-crème - deigned to accept posts there, and these in the more salubrious climes of East Africa, and both for entirely different reasons. One of them was a keen big-game hunter, and the other a collector - one might call

---

[15] Indian Civil Service

him a bargain hunter - and thus they were given the opportunity to indulge in their hobbies.

Now, I am no angel myself, and I confess that I have always preferred a European or North American posting to any other. I was greatly upset, therefore, when one fine morning, sitting comfortably at my desk in Mexico City at an elevation of 7,000+ feet and with snow-capped Mount Popocatepetl forming a pleasing backdrop, my secretary brought me the cipher message informing me of my transfer to Nigeria. In the bag the same day the Foreign Secretary wrote to tell me that P.N. Haksar, my predecessor, had done a fine job at Lagos, that it was a challenging assignment, and that he felt sure that I would rise to the occasion. As a sop, he added: "We have asked for formal agreement for your concurrent accreditation as Ambassador to Togo, Dahomey and Cameroon." I had been hoping for a transfer to Vienna; and for weeks thereafter I trudged in the slough of despond.

But ours not to question why: So three months later my wife and I were on the Middle East Airlines plane that came down at Ikeja airport at four or five or some such unearthly hour in the morning. As we came down the ramp, the heat was stifling and the humidity - well, I have never encountered anything quite so oppressive. We were whisked away to a lounge by the Chief of Protocol and while we waited for our luggage to be cleared, we were surrounded by a hundred or so of our compatriots, some of them carrying garlands, and I remember wondering why the flowers had not wilted more than they had done

We had settled in well, when one day the President of the Hindustani Majlis[16] came to see me. "Your Excellency", he said. "As you know, we try to keep abreast of things taking place at home. That is why, apart from the facilities available in the Mission's library, we subscribe to several Indian newspapers and magazines. Last year we donated, through Your Excellency, the equivalent of a lakh of rupees to alleviate the distress of flood victims in Marakhauli. We are anxious at all times to prove our oneness with the soil from which we are sprung."

That was not only a fine speech; it was indeed the case. Indian communities everywhere are proud of their origin and, with but a few exceptions, go out of their way to preserve the culture and traditions

---

[16] Hindustani Council.

of their forbears. I have been associated with such groups in Panama, Nigeria, Sudan and Indonesia, and I can testify to the fact.

"Motilalji", I told him, "Your loyalty is well known. I have often had occasion to compliment you on the interest you take in the causes of the motherland and in the welfare of the community that has so properly elected you as their leader in this country. I need no reminder. What has happened to make you approach me at this time?"

"Excellency", he replied, shuffling in his seat, "I have been reading about this thing called population explosion. Panditji has said that all Indians should unite to curb the undue growth of their families. For this purpose we held a meeting the other day and formed a committee to devise ways and means to further our national objective. The members are waiting outside and would like to have a word with you".

He brought them in. One of them was a bachelor from the Punjab, a strapping Sikh who was returning to Bhatinda in a few weeks to bring himself a bride. Another was a gentleman from Uttar Pradesh who had four wives and twice that number of children but, forced by the pressure on his present accommodation, was contemplating sending most of them back to his village near Allahabad. The third was from Kerala; his great sorrow was that, although happily married for twelve years, he had not so far been blessed with a child.

They beamed at me, their smiles spreading from wall to wall as they told me of their desire to contribute to the common effort. One point they made was the ineffectiveness of Government publicity methods. They mentioned something Gandhiji had once said: "There are enough slaves in India – why produce more?" This had inspired them with their own slogan, "India Wants Fewer Mouths To Feed." What did I think of it?

I told them that slogans were alright in the right place and at the right time, and that theirs sounded okay, but there was still much work that remained to be done. They nodded their heads comprehendingly, finished their cups of tea, shook my hand and promised to let me know as soon as their efforts began to make an impact.

They never reported to me again, and when I asked Motilal about the matter some twelve months later, he shook his head sadly. "The committee has been disbanded" he told me. "The members said they couldn't get any cooperation". He went on to say that Shival Singh was now the proud father of twins, that Maula Baksh would soon be able to field a hockey eleven made up of his own progeny, and that George Abraham had at long last been blessed with a son and heir.

*

The politeness of kings

At a very early age my father impressed on me the importance of punctuality. "L'exactitude est la politesse des rois," he would say in his rusting French, a smattering of which he had picked up in Europe at the time he was called to the Bar. "The politeness of kings," he would repeat, translating for my benefit. "The British have done many cruel things to our country, but they have taught us some good things too. Amongst these I place punctuality foremost. Please to remember this, my boy. Punctuality is the politeness of kings."

I was often to be reminded of this sermon during my time in Latin America. When we arrived in Mexico City, for example, the neighbours overwhelmed us with their kindness. A basket of flowers from across the road. A brace of pheasants from the people next door. A Spanish-English phrase-book from our landlord.

We quickly settled in, and my wife decided that it was time to become better acquainted. As our engraved cards had arrived from the printers, each one embossed with the Ashoka emblem in gold, she issued formal invitations for our modest first party – "Tea at 5 o'clock. Repondez s'il vous plait." She had taught the cook how to make pakodas and samosas, but she herself made the sandwiches, watercress, cucumber, ham, chicken, and from the bakery at the end of our street she ordered the most appetizing cakes and pastries imaginable. We had brought with us a special blend of Darjeeling tea - there was coffee besides, of course - and the official crockery gleamed in the afternoon sun trickling through the bay windows. On a side table a variety of wines and spirits awaited those who might indicate such preference.

Five o'clock came and then five-thirty. At six we decided that we might as well allow ourselves a cup of tea. Six-thirty, yet nobody had arrived. We checked the calendar but, no, this was the appointed day, and the replies indicated that our invitations had been duly received and accepted in writing. Had we done something to offend the neighbourhood? At seven we ordered that the spread should be removed.

Dejectedly, our teenage daughters took off their party clothes and began to prepare for bed. I poured myself a whisky and switched on the television. Amidst the racket of an American gangster film, the doorbell sounded and our first guests arrived. Soon the drawing-room was buzzing with people in animated conversation. All those we had invited were present, and they tackled the food with considerable gusto, uttering such remarks as "Que sabroso!" and "Que delicioso!" but not one word of apology or explanation. Soon we were to learn that this was the custom, señor; and, sometimes, a good thing, too, as I shall proceed to explain.

Some months later, Jawaharlal Nehru arrived on his first (and only) visit to Latin America. His first official engagement was an address to a joint session of Parliament, immediately preceding a luncheon he was to give in honour of President Lopez Mateos and members of his Cabinet. Before going to the, rostrum he asked me in Hindi, "How long should I speak?" and I replied, "An hour or forty-five minutes." He toyed with his wristwatch, adjusted the rose in his achkan and mounted the podium.

Forty-five minutes went by, and then an hour, and I looked anxiously at Mrs. Gandhi, seated on the floor of the House with Mr. M. J. Desai, then our Foreign Secretary. The barest minimum of time was left for the banquet he was hosting for the Head of State, but the Prime Minister gave no sign of ending his speech. I left the chamber hurriedly and made some frantic telephone calls. "No se preocupe, Señor Embajador" I was told. "Think nothing of it. Señor Presidente and los Ministros will have lunch at three instead of two." As simple as that.

The Prime Minister's speech lasted exactly an hour and forty-five minutes. He looked at his wristwatch with a satisfied smile, descended from the dais amidst a standing ovation, and we left the House as if nothing untoward had happened.

The luncheon was an outstanding success. I still have a copy of the menu, and it would fill this page. As a gesture towards his guests, the Prime Minister had agreed that wine should be served, and this was noticed and appreciated. Responding to the toast, the President lauded India, paying tribute to Mr. Nehru's policies in the pursuit of world peace. No one even mentioned the fact that a delay had taken place. The punctuality of Kings or the politeness of Presidents, I asked myself, which was the better of the two?

*

Little things that never happen

Suddenly they switched, from the sublime to the ridiculous, in a manner of speaking. A moment ago they had been discussing, among a dozen other things, the future of Bangladesh and the implications of Nixon's visit to Peking, but now they applied themselves to an examination of the state of the union - our Union, that is, Bharat. Then one of them turned to me. He wore a khadi cap and Jawahar jacket made of coarse homespun materials. He peered into my eyes through horn-rimmed spectacles and asked: "What are the things that annoy you most?"

I had met them after a long time - twenty years or more. They were my friends and some of them had been to college with me. They were anxious to know how I was readjusting to "the new life" after my lengthy sojourn in different parts of the world. The one in the white topi pinned me down. He had resigned a senior job in one of the corporations and now described himself as a social worker. "Come on, man, tell us about the things that really get your goat," he insisted.

I raised what might be described as a quizzical eyebrow. I was their guest and had agreed to kick around with them, but I was not prepared for an inquisition nor did I want to become involved in a controversy, so I compromised. "I agree there's still a lot of leeway to be made up," I mumbled vaguely, and added: "But give it a coat of paint and it'll be all right." That didn't satisfy them but they got the message and they switched back to matters of greater import - the Malthusian theory of population control, to be precise.

But I chewed on that question for a long time. What are the things most annoying to a person returning to his homeland after a prolonged absence abroad? And then I made a simple discovery. Apart from matters of national policy, about which the individual and local bodies can't do much anyway, the things that really get one down are - the things that don't get done: the garbage that never gets collected, the repairman who never arrives, the letters that remain unacknowledged, the parcels that are never delivered, the telephone that rings but is never answered.

Early in my career I started dealings with a bank of noble lineage, one of those establishments which have escaped nationalisation in our country and which, although its name has been changed for administrative reasons, still maintains its links with one of the Big Five in London. Alas, not only has the name changed, but the service too. After months of protracted correspondence, all one way, to obtain a simple statement of account, in exasperation I wrote an angry letter to the big white chief. At last I got a reply: "We regret to inform you that we do not appear to have received your recent communications." But managed to get that statement.

That venerable institution, the Life Insurance Corporation, specialises in this very kind of thing. I sent them payment for an annual premium about a month before the due date. The weeks went by and when, despite several reminders, I still got no reply, I resorted to what has become my favourite ploy - I wrote fiercely in protest to the boss man. Promptly I received an acknowledgement, a "suspense memorandum", from which I gathered that, although I had given the number of my policy in each one of my letters, they were still trying to "locate" my account. Some days later I got an official receipt - sent to an address I had changed much earlier and which, they had assured me, had been noted in our books.'

The same sorry story, I regret to say, repeats itself, with but slight variations, in the office of the Accountant-General, the Post Office, the public utilities corporations and almost every sector of our everyday life - a tale of routine payments delayed for quibbling reasons ("Your bill is returned unpaid as it should be signed with a proper pen"), parcels languishing or pilfered, and rubble which turns from a mound into a mountain before your very eyes. We have a genius for procrastination and we have developed prevarication into a fine art.

There's a pile of garbage a few yards down the street on which I live. It stagnates at the very entrance to the residential executive suites of one of our major companies, whose main headquarters building is adjoining. For years now I've watched it grow in size and dimension, coconut husks mingling with egg shells and rotting vegetables, a playground for pariah dogs and vultures and sewer rats; it swarms with flies, and its stench rises to high heaven. Nobody seems very much concerned, and an enterprising fellow has even opened an al-fresco restaurant alongside, to which taxi-drivers and passing peons flock at all hours of the day.

Outside Calcutta's New Market is a sign which almost screams at all comers: "Dogs Not Allowed." Yet the mangiest of creatures freely roam between the stalls of the meat section and are even thrown chunks of unwanted flesh and bones by the kind-hearted vendors. A European visitor noticed this discrepancy on a day when a pye-bitch was on heat, making the scene nastier than ever. She questioned my wife, who in turn questioned one of the stall-keepers. "Kya Karun mensahib"[17] he replied. He admitted that an Inspector made a periodical round as required by the regulations, but after this worthy had pocketed his tribute of a few rupees, he lost all further interest.

Other unnecessary harassments abound. Why, for example, does the well-heeled theatre proprietor abandon all form of ventilation (not only the air-conditioning) as soon as the cooler weather approaches, rendering his crowded cinema hall more stifling and uncomfortable than any Black Hole? And why are expensive eating places so miserly in their use of disinfectant in their pokey wash-rooms? And why must so many man-holes remain open and unprotected, veritable death-traps for the unsuspecting passer-by? And why must shops encroach on the pavements outside their premises, and why must every public hydrant become a bathing ghat for the entire servant population of the area? And why...

Some people tend to explain away such matters by saying that we are a large country, and poor, and other problems are more compelling. Yet in other newly independent countries, some of them more under-developed than ourselves, laws have been passed, and are enforced, prohibiting nuisances of the kind described. On our own continent, in nearby Singapore and Malaysia, spitting, begging and the spreading of

---

[17] "What shall we do?"

litter, and urinating and defecating in public places, are offences which invoke heavy penalties and have been eliminated by ruthless application of the regulations. Why are we, alone amongst the populations of the world, so backward insofar as civic responsibility and discipline are concerned?

I remember arriving in an African capital to find an uprooted oak tree straddling the entrance to our bungalow, following an overnight storm. Half an hour after a single telephone call, a Municipality truck arrived and a gang removed the offending trunk. Not only that, they moved right along the road and cleared the entire thoroughfare of scattered leaves, shrubs and assorted rubble.

Later in the day I visited the bank where our embassy maintained its account, a subsidiary of the same institution which caused me the trouble mentioned earlier in this narrative. The clerk gave me a form to fill, and within minutes she handed me a cheque-book with my name and the number of my account neatly stamped on all its pages. When I thanked her, her white teeth lighted up a face carved in pure ebony. "It was a pleasure, sir," she replied, adding that a statement would be sent to me in the first week of every month. That promise was scrupulously observed, and I never had occasion to lodge a complaint of any kind. Just try and get a bank clerk do anything for you with a smile in any of our nationalised establishments!

Some months ago, (before the Emergency) as I was putting the finishing touches to this manuscript, there was a knock on the door of my study and the postman presented me with a small parcel and a receipt slip for my signature. This was quite an event, as all the gift parcels sent recently by our daughters abroad have simply not arrived. This one was sealed with wax and string and bore the imprint of the Customs Department, promising at least that its contents were safe. We opened it eagerly, and found it - empty! Not one of the half-dozen small items, duly declared and within the permissible limit, had been spared. I reported this matter to the Postmaster-General the same day, and sent another protest in reminder - but in our great country in this day and age, what are complaints but mere straws in the wind?

I related all this to my Gandhi-capped friend, the social worker, when I saw him next, and suggested that strewn amongst these experiences might perhaps be the answer to his earlier question. My idea of Utopia, I told him, was a land not necessarily flowing with milk and honey, but one in which the people had a pride in what they were doing and a desire to make things work. As things were, I said, there was a sort of anarchy in many of our major undertakings. Nobody knew if anything worked well and, what was worse, nobody seemed to care. Why was this, I asked.

My friend removed his topi and scratched his balding pate. Then he took a strip of tinfoil out of his jacket pocket and extracted two tablets, which he proceeded to swallow. He pushed the strip in my direction; it was stamped with the name of a well-known brand of tranquiliser. "Have one", he invited me. "Or better still, have two."

6

On the family

The character of the people who surround you are of utmost importance – only they can support, advise and maintain decorum in the pandemonium that is diplomatic life. Let me illustrate with some excellent examples from within my own family.

Waste not, want not

Kamla was my favourite aunt. The oldest of my father's widowed sisters, she had never seen the inside of a classroom, yet she possessed the wisdom of the ages. Waste not, want not, she used to tell me in her own vernacular translation, and throughout the years of a somewhat spendthrift life, those words have haunted me.

Aunt Kamla was only thirty five at the time, but she looked like a woman of sixty. Each morning she would sit on a small wooden stool not far removed from the kitchen, a tattered copy of the Bhagavad-Gita on her lap, a pair of cheap steel-rimmed spectacles perched on her nose, muttering verse after verse – yet she couldn't read a word. Her gnarled forefinger would trace each line, and at the end of the each half-hour session, radiance would illuminate her countenance as she prepared to face whatever the day might bring.

When I first went abroad, she was twenty years older but, apart from her hair which was now snow-white, she hadn't changed a bit. "Ka-Ka", she said to me (though I was now a man, she still called me "child"), "you are about to start a new life. There will be much excitement and pleasure, but there will also be pitfalls. I am a wrinkled old woman now and you will soon forget me, and then I will be gone forever, but take heed of what I have taught you. Waste not and you will want not – there is no greater joy than contentment." Then she pressed me to her ample bosom and I could feel the cold tears trickling down my spine.

"Kamli (silly) auntie" I teased her, enjoying the pun on her name. "How can I ever forget you? And where on earth do you think you'll be when I come home every other year? You're not going any place at all – just be sure you're right here when I come next time and again and again."

I'm afraid I wasn't a good prophet, because Aunt Kamla died two months later, nor was I much of a pupil, as I've always spent way beyond my means. On that first trip, on the P&O liner "Stratheden", when other people were doling out shillings at bingo, I was losing pounds at poker on a green topped table in a smoke filled card room, and while they visited the sights and tea-rooms at the various ports of call, I was looking up nightclubs and cabarets. No wonder that when we docked at Tilbury I didn't have as much as a penny in the little purse my aunt had given me.

As I said, her words have haunted me, and in my travels around the world I have tried every now and again to economize in some way or another – by cutting down on my smoking, by buying a less expensive brand of whisky or by going to a cheaper tailor. None of these sacrifices lasted more than a week or two. No, I am not a strong-willed man.

In the winter of one's life, one becomes a little wiser and less brash, and I have often wondered how much better off I might be if I had heeded Aunt Kamla's advice.

*

Diplomatic passport

One time my wife was returning to London after spending a weekend with me in Paris, where I was attached to our delegation to the third session of the United Nations General Assembly. This was at Hendon – Heathrow Airport was still only a plan on a drawing-board. It was cold and dank and altogether quite miserable, more woebegone than even Dum Dum before the new terminal building came up.

She got through the first desk quickly enough. The trouble started at the next stop.

"That coat, madam?"

"It's Russian squirrel."

"I know it is" said the man, "but where did you get it?"

"In Canada last year" said my wife.

He scratched his head. This was a fine how-do-you-do – an Indian traveller from France arriving in Britain with a Russian fur coat purchased in Canada! Something bloody fishy going on there. "Oi, Fred" he said, beckoning to his twin at the adjoining counter. The two got into a huddle. My wife twiddled her thumbs. Outside it was raining cats and dogs.

"That coat, madam?" said the new man.

"It's Russian squirrel and I bought it in Canada last year."

"Could I see the receipt, please?"

"The receipt? Don't be ridiculous. I never carry such things around with me."

"I'm sorry, madam, but you'll have to leave the coat behind until you can produce satisfactory evidence."

The little lady exploded. "Receipts?! Leave the coat behind?! Produce satisfactory evidence?! Is that how you people treat visitors with diplomatic passports?"

"Diplomatic passport?" He picked up the booklet lying neglected on the counter. "I'm most awfully sorry, madam. There's been such a lot of smuggling going on since the war, you know." He turned to his mate. "The lady can go through now, Bill."

Bill was himself examining the passport for the first time, studying the picture page with serious intent.

"But it's not the same lady" he said at last. "Here, Fred, have a dekko."

Fred had a dekko. "This isn't your photo, madam."

"Of course it's my photo. It looks a little different because I had my hair done in Paris."

She gave them a look.

They let the lady go.

*

The great jewel robbery

We had recently arrived from Canada on my transfer to India House in London, when one morning I saw on my desk a large envelope gold-embossed with the sovereign's coat-of-arms and containing the Lord Chamberlain's compliments, etc. All senior officers of foreign and commonwealth missions are usually invited to one or other of the Royal garden parties, so it wasn't such a special thing as might appear.

Our first concern was what to wear. Friends told me that, for the first time since the war, Moss Bros. were again renting out toppers and cutaway coats, but the very idea of hired clothes revolted me. Likewise, I refused to wear black achkan and churidars, as by nature I am a modest man and try hard not to look conspicuous. Finally I settled on a charcoal-grey lounge suit I'd had made in Saville Row some weeks earlier. This and a club tie, plus wing-tipped black brogues by Victor, and my outfit was complete.

My wife's case was simpler. She still had a Benares sari, given to her when we were married, which she'd hardly worn because it was "too much" but which seemed just right for this occasion. To supplement it was a fur coat, a Russian squirrel I'd bought for her when we were in Montreal. And from a mail-order firm I'd got her a string of imitation pearls, advertised as Ciro's or some other such name, which when concealed under the folds of her sari, and in the fading light, could be mistaken for the real McCoy.

I have never been particularly partial to baubles or precious metals; and neither – praise the Lord! – has my wife. So far as she was concerned, they were worth a million dollars. When she was all decked up, even though I say so myself, no maharani could hold a candle to her, she looked like a wealthy heiress from the fabled East.

We arrived in proper style, as I had requisitioned one of India House's chauffeured Austin Princesses, on condition that I would release it on arrival and make my own way home. The Guardsmen in their busbies remained frozen at attention as we passed through the main gates of the palace and followed the long line converging on to the emerald green lawns. The military bands played in the distance.

Their majesties were all graciousness, mingling among their guests, a smile for everyone and a handshake for some, followed by the two Princesses, one of whom is now Queen of England. In the crowd of maybe two thousand, we spotted the cherubic face of Winston Churchill and, some paces away, his successor, Clement Attlee, whose sedate appearance was a reminder of the former's remark in the House of Commons: "The honourable gentleman is but a sheep in sheep's clothing." Then we were overtaken by a succession of old India hands we knew.

First there was Field Marshall Lord Auchinleck, bowler-hatted now, who had been Commander-in-Chief when I had done my brief wartime stint. Then Sir Eric Bozman, who had been Secretary of Information and Broadcasting, in the company of Sir Percival Griffiths, principal organiser of the National War Front. Then Alan Cambell-Johnson, who had been Lord Mountbatten's Press Attaché, sauntered along and led us to the buffet tables.

There were cucumber and watercress sandwiches, sausage rolls, cream puffs and steaming cups of tea – why do the English make better tea than we do in India? – and although there might have been some variety at other tables, we stayed in one place until Their Majesties left and the band played 'God save the King.' We then followed the crowd, wended our way up the Horse Guards Parade in the direction of Trafalgar Square, and were lucky to find a free taxi.

A short way from home, my wife clutched at her throat and cried: "My pearls – they're gone!" She looked inside the folds of her sari and felt around the seat of the cab but, no, they were nowhere to be found. I tried to cheer her up. "They only cost ten dollars" I reminded her; but my wife is a sentimental person. "You gave them to me for my birthday" she reproached me, a hurt look in her eyes.

The evening paper was lying on our doorstep and on the front page the headline shrieked: "Jewel Thieves Strike Again!" The report went on to describe how the Lady So-and-So had reported the loss of her sapphire bracelet after attending a soiree the night before, and how in the morning thieves had broken into the suite of a visiting American millionaire and decamped with his wife's jewellery box.

We just hoped the thief wasn't too disappointed with us.

*

From the mouths of babes

A group of us at India House got together to give a farewell luncheon to R.S. (Tom) Mani, the genial Deputy High Commissioner, who was being transferred to another post. In this party were Arthur S. Lall, the Commercial Secretary, and Professor Sundaram, the Education Secretary, and also Captain Srinivasan and Prithi Singh, Private Secretaries to the High Commissioner, and Jamal Kid-wai, my No. 2 in the Public Relations Department. Alas, Tom Mani and the Professor are no more, the former having died during secondment to the United Nations, and the latter while serving another stint in the UK under Mrs Pandit.

It was an expensive meal. Although there wasn't much to choose in the way of food in those post-war London days, for some strange reason there was no restriction on the sale of potables, and what we might have missed in solid fare we more than made up in the liquid department. I don't quite remember what exactly we ordered, but I do remember that we imbibed a lot and that I mixed my drinks into the bargain, and that when I returned to the office I had the father and mother of all sick headaches.

There was no question of any further work for me that afternoon, so I asked for a staff car to take me home and telephoned my wife to tell her about my condition. The chauffeur doffed his peaked cap, clicked his heels and gave me an anxious look as I clambered into the gleaming Austin Princess. Somewhere along the Strand I pulled a travelling rug over my legs, and, by way of explanation, told the driver that I thought I'd had another attack of malaria, which malady (I continued) had bedevilled me since childhood. He gave a grunt of sympathy, dodged a double-decker bus and steered his way through other motley vehicles.

We had passed Hampstead. I was still pressing my throbbing head and moaning silently when, during a lull in the traffic, the driver turned around and said: "Can be the very devil, that malaria, sir – the amount of kwai-nine they pumped into me at Burma is nobody's business" and he was telling me about "that new wonder drug atta-bryne" when he pulled up outside our house in Tenterden Gardens. The front door opened, and there stood my six-year-old daughter Rowena, her arms akimbo, a frown wrinkling her brow. She yelled at me from across the lawn:

"You shouldn't drink so much, Daddy!"

The chauffeur kept a straight face.

*

My man Sumatra

Sumatra was a legacy. When I arrived in Lahore, he was just handed over to me with other domestic goods and chattels. He had been employed by my predecessors as a sort of general factotum and in the same capacity by his predecessors ever since independence.

How he got the name I never knew. What I did know was that one of the biggest islands of the Indonesian archipelago was so named and that I had visited its capital, Medan, some months earlier when I was in charge of the mission at Djakarta.

When I stepped out of the house on my first day in office, Sumatra was diligently rubbing the bonnet of the car, attempting to erase an offensive but entirely imaginary stain, the Delhi-based chauffeur looking on indulgently. Suddenly he dropped the polishing cloth, snapped me a salute that would have done credit to a sergeant-major, and opened the door for me.

That was my first encounter with Sumatra, and it was several months before I learned something about his background. During the Quetta earth-quake, when he was a boy, his entire family had been wiped out, buried inside the ruins of their miserable hutment – mother, father, three brothers and four sisters. He himself escaped because he was visiting an aunt in another village. On that day, he vowed to Allah that never would he make an attachment with a human being whose life could be snuffed out at a moment's notice.

My senior officers warned me that Sumatra was a spy, an informer, someone planted by the authorities to report all goings-on at the residence. If he was a spy, I told them, I wish they made more like him. He was hard-working, efficient, resourceful – and loyal.

When I prowled the house in the middle of the night, unable to sleep because of some problem or another that had arisen during the day – relations between our two countries were at a low ebb – Sumatra would be there at a discreet distance, awaiting my slightest wish or command. And once he actually brought me, without me asking him, a bottle of aspirin and a glass of water, and he urged me: "Take two of these, Sahib…"

Our spaniel "Gypsy" took to him like a fish to water, and when at dawn we wondered where he had disappeared, we would find him later, huddled up inside the rags of Sumatra's charpoy. When the dog fell ill, Sumatra carried him in his arms to the vet; and when the mongrel died of distemper, he went about with swollen red eyes for at least a day.

When our daughters arrived on holiday from their school in Darjeeling, he became their self-appointed guide and devoted nanny. Nothing was too much to do for him. He ran around in circles executing their pettiest errands.

No hours were too long for him, no task too distasteful. He, alone of all the servants, would sit in a corner outside the drawing-room, awaiting the departure of the last guest after a prolonged bridge session; and when someone became sick, as they sometimes did after too much food or drink, he dealt with the situation with considerable professionalism.

A year and a bit later, the tricolour atop the residence was hauled down for the last time, the result of a series of complicated reciprocal manoeuvres whereby a number of posts in India and Pakistan were ordered to close. When the flag was folded and brought to me, he rushed forward and raised the hem to his forehead, in full view of high local officials and the honour guard attending the ceremony.

The other day I had a letter from an old friend in Lahore. He had just come back from burying one of his retainers, he wrote, and the reason he was writing was because in the man's belongings they had found a photograph of me and my family and several snapshots of a long haired dog, one of them in my company. The man's name was Sumatra, the letter said.

*

A man of two worlds

Algernon Blackwood was in India during the war holding down a cushy job at GHQ - moving little coloured flags up and down a wall map or stamping permits, that kind of thing. He was the nephew of a Viscount or an Earl, I forget which, and I thought it quite out of character for him to be so far away from the fighting when most of his breed were in the thick of the action everywhere. Then someone told me that he had been wounded in the retreat from Dunkirk and was still listed as an invalid. The crown on his epaulettes identified him as a Major.

I was mixed up in those days with an outfit called the War Services Exhibition, a sort of circus travelling from this metropolis to that State capital, spending a month or six weeks in each. It was something designed to stimulate recruiting and promote the war effort; and was given such high priority that all doors in the Government were open to us. Nobody less than a Governor or a Maharaja was invited to perform each opening, and special trains carried our equipment from one place to another. Altogether we had a whale of a time.

Algernon was in the group that accompanied the C-in-C when the exhibition opened in Delhi's Ram Lila grounds. I was in the escorting party and found myself next to him for most of the time. He walked with a slight limp and, when he spoke, he stuttered and had the habit of blinking his pale blue eyes - the result of shell shock, I was told. When we were done for the day, I asked him if he would join us for a drink at the Imperial; and that's when our friendship began.

Thereafter Algernon made it a point to be present at all our openings, and he followed us methodically - Bombay after Delhi, and then Bangalore, Madras and the whole gamut. On these occasions he spent the night with us wherever we were camped (in fancy hotels mainly or State guest houses), and on that special night we painted the town red - or a shade of pink, in deference to prevailing regulations. "G-gosh, I f-feel such a heel", he said once after one of those bashes. "The cream of England's youth and talent dying on battlefields the world over, and look at me - hundreds of miles from nowhere, a ph-phoney, a f-fraud with a limp and a f-fountain pen". A medical board had just pronounced him unfit for further active duty.

The war ended and I forgot all about Algernon until one night in London while coming out of the Haymarket theatre into the pouring rain with not the ghost of a chance of finding a taxi, I heard a shout: "Hey, Pete!" I looked in the direction of the voice, wondering who in Blighty would know my wartime nickname, when there was Algernon Blackwood, leaning across a good-looking brunette to hold open the door of a purring Rolls-Royce Silver Cloud. "Hop in", he commanded. "Move over a bottle. Oh, by the way Melissa, this is Pete. Pete, Melissa." His stutter seemed much improved.

We proceeded to one of those new apartment blocks in Mayfair, somewhere in the vicinity of the Hilton and Londonderry hotels – top-hatted doorman, striped awning, potted palms, concealed lighting and jaunty liftboys in pillbox hats. We got off at the eighth floor and entered a flat which was elegant but none too large or fancy – with a lovely view of Hyde Park. En route I had learned that Melissa and Algernon were man and wife, that she was Greek and that they had been married for seven years, with their first child on the way. Further, that the uncle, the Earl or the Viscount, had lost his only son in a plane crash in the month after the war and that the title and estate and all that went with them had come to Algernon as next-of-kin.

After taxes, it didn't amount to all that much, he told me, but he still had a million or two to play around with. Besides, he was on the board of a half-dozen city corporations on whose behalf he travelled hither and yon, mostly to the Americas, so it wasn't such a bad life. "Not flush, old boy", he said blinking his pale blue eyes, "but comfortable, I'd say – moderately comfortable."

He switched on the hi-fi. It was an Indian classical recording, and he looked at me as if asking for my approval, but I'm a complete heathen so far as classical stuff is concerned, Indian or foreign, so I avoided his gaze and examined the sleeve of the L.P., from which I gathered that this was a combination of many talents, among those of Yehudi Menuhin, Ravi Shankar and Ustad Ali Akbar Kahn.

Meanwhile, Melissa returned with a tray laden with smoked salmon, caviar, pate de foie gras, pieces of Melba toast and little blobs of butter. Algernon went to the bar and dropped chunks of ice in glasses half-filled with his favourite brand of whisky. I winced. In the old days we used to berate the Yanks for spoiling good Scotch in this manner. He noticed this and apologised. "Picked up the filthy habit in the States, and it's stuck, dammit." Then he announced that we would go to his club for dinner. "Boodles – the very best and oldest in London town."

Some Londoners will challenge that statement. Boodles is by no means the best nor by a long shot the oldest of its thousand and one clubs, but it does have something – call it atmosphere or tradition or what you will. Their staff wear an attire that is no different from any of the others and their accent is about the same, but they show a deference, a willingness to please that puts them in a class apart. They are just right. The night I was there with the Blackwoods, I felt I was in pre-war England – so steeped is the place in the qualities I have mentioned. The food was only so-so, but the service was superb, which tended to accentuate the disappointments I had experienced during my current tour. Good manners, it seemed, were fast disappearing from this nation of shopkeepers. Where once the customer was always right, now nobody cared less. No wonder they're losing out to the competition, I mused, and the thought saddened me because, whatever the past, or perhaps because of it, Indians still have a soft corner for the British and wish them well.

We were having one last Drambuie. I was catching an early plane for Lagos and, despite their protestations, I wanted to present myself at my next post in a decent enough condition, for which some sleep was necessary. Suddenly the room became silent.

I looked at Algernon and raised my glass. "Here's looking at you", I told him, "and wishing that it won't be another twenty years before we meet again." He blinked his pale blue eyes, and I went on: "From what I can see, you have everything a man can desire. Tell me Algy, are you happy?"

He cleared his throat, fiddled with the stem of his glass and looked at Melissa for encouragement. "Give my regards to your chaps back in Delhi and Bombay", he said at last. "I had some rattling good times with them. But tell them this from me." He paused as if searching for words. "When the time comes – as come it must – for your people to lose their cooks and their bearers, they'll feel truly bereaved, as I still feel bereaved." He swallowed some more. "As you say, I have mostly everything, yes, but I'd be a lot happier if I had Mustafa here with me. Mustafa was a wonderful chap, a khidmatgar without peer – produced meals fit for a king with no notice at all. Kept my shoes shining like mirrors and the creases of my trousers sharp as a razor. They don't make people like Mustafa any more, not even your side of Suez."

Algernon wasn't given to flippancy, but now he raised four fingers of his right hand and touched them to his forehead, bowing slightly, "Sahib, Sahib", he said, "Give my regards too to the Mustafas that remain."

*

Say it with flowers

A nice old custom is to send flowers to convey one's good wishes on festive occasions – marriages, births, anniversaries and the like. How or when the practice began it is difficult to say, but certain it is that in days of yore Anthony used to dispatch bargefuls of orchids to Cleopatra to commemorate their meeting and to proclaim his undying love and fealty.

In the diplomatic corps, it is de rigueur for an Ambassador to send baskets of flowers to their colleagues on their National Days. That's all very nice; but it can be an expensive business. When I was in Mexico, there were more than a hundred other embassies and legations in the capital, which meant that it was incumbent on me to purchase an average of ten floral offerings a month. With the price around two hundred pesos per bouquet – about a hundred rupees – this could have been quite a strain on my modest frais de representation.

I was lucky, however. Shortly after I arrived, I was sent a new Private Secretary, T. Vembu Nair by name, a really first-class chap who, in addition to the usual proficiencies, had a sort of public relations manner which made him get on with even the most impossible people.

One morning I sent Nair to the florist on the ground floor of our office building to select an arrangement of gladioli and carnations for the Ethiopian Minister, and when my wife saw it at the reception later in the day, she was so pleased that she asked me to let my assistant do this chore for her on similar future occasions.

On the third or fourth time, I noticed that the bill had suddenly come down by half, and I asked Nair about this. He gave me a shy smile and then told me how he had struck up a friendship with Señor Sanchez, the florist, who was giving him a special discount – "solamente para su pais", "only for your country."

It seems that when Señor Sanchez was coming down his ladder on the day of Nair's first visit, he was seized by a violent constriction of the back, caused by an old affliction. There was nobody else in the shop at the time, so Nair had made the old man lie down on a bench and had massaged him back to normalcy. This was when Nair told the florist about the healing properties of yoga, and he was invited to demonstrate his prowess after dinner at the Sanchez home.

Hernando Sanchez, a widower, was looked after by his daughter, Carmen, who had herself lost her husband in a factory explosion some years earlier. She was plump and soft, a sloe-eyed, auburn-haired beauty. Nair was dark as the night, but that sort of thing doesn't amount to much in countries like Mexico, and when he stripped off for his yoga exercises he revealed the physique of a 'Mr Universe' contestant. The two of them fell for each other – strictly platonic, of course – and when Hernando's ailment was cured, Nair became their yoga instructor and a regular visitor to their home. Hence the discount.

Even without a frais de representation these days, one must send flowers to friends from time to time. With the cost of living what it is, this can hurt. At such times I think of T. Vembu Nair, and if he happens to read these lines he will know how much I appreciated his services.

*

Eddie the Basset

Eddie is a basset hound and he's thirteen years old – which means that, in terms of human beings, he's in his nineties. No wonder he has slowed down so much, snaps at all and sundry, and wants to sleep all day and all night, unless its time to eat.

He belonged originally to our daughter Aruna and her husband Elie. When they got married and were allotted a chalet in Lagos near the Ikeja airport, they thought it might be a smart idea to have a watchdog around, as it was a somewhat lonely neighbourhood. So they got the pick of the litter from an American friend and promptly named him Eddie after Elie's boss, Edwin. Then they got transferred to Las Palmas and asked if we would be good parents-in-law and take over the little fellow.

We did; and I must say that Elie had done a good job training Eddie. He never made any mess inside the house, was always romping around the tennis courts, jumping in and out of the lagoon that surrounded the place, minding his own business and scaring the living daylights out of anyone who looked like an intruder. We really got attached to the rascal, and when we ourselves got transferred, we had the cutest bassinet made so that he could travel with us in proper style.

But the airline people would have none of this, and they put him in the luggage compartment with our other paraphernalia. When we got out at the other end, Eddie had shrunk to half his size and he looked up at us with a complaining look that seemed to say: "How could you do such a thing to me?" On top of this a terrific haboob came up on the day of our arrival: those storms that used to come up from the desert and bring with them all the sands of the Sahara. Eddie whined the whole night through, and we thought he would die. In the morning our friend Sunder Singh brought in the vet, who gave him a sedative.

Despite the trauma, Eddie grew into quite a lad, the Casanova of our community and my own personal hero. Late one afternoon I came home from playing tennis with our next-door neighbour, the Yugoslav Ambassador, Gojko Zarcovic, when I found a newly arrived pile of papers from India lying on one of the tables of our drawing-room overlooking the Blue Nile. I tossed off my sneakers, propped my feet up on the table and asked Mustafa, the steward, to bring me some tea. I was engrossed in the latest scandal from Delhi when Eddie started barking excitedly and running around in circles. I yelled at him to shut up, and then threw a magazine at him, all to no avail.

Exasperated, I was about to step into my shoes, when there, curling up from inside the laces, was a foot-long krait, its grooved fangs darting in and out viciously and staring me right in the face. I shouted for the servants and they swiftly killed him, and later told us that it had been one of Africa's most poisonous snakes and that, but for the grace of God and Eddie's warning antics, I would have been a sure goner.

When we retired and came back to India, he couldn't quite understand why we didn't have tennis courts or lagoons or fruit trees surrounding the house. I never did listen to my aunt Kamla. All we've got now is a dried-up fish pond not much larger than our bathtub. There isn't much garden space either, but Eddie's got used to what we have, and so have we.

ACKNOWLEDGEMENTS

We would like to thank a number of people for their help and support in the production of this book:

Lynne Brooke for his thoughtfulness and support.

Rowena Sagrani for her patience and humour.

Marta Muñoz for the brilliant artwork.

Andy Park for the excellent graphic design.

Finally, but by no means least, the members of the book group who gave invaluable feedback and support in the last stages of production:

Bernadette Hawkes

Katrina Finch

Alison Walker

Anna Mojak